## BFI Film Classics

The BFI Film Classics series introduces, interprets and celebrates landmarks of world cinema. Each volume offers an argument for the film's 'classic' status, together with discussion of its production and reception history, its place within a genre or national cinema, an account of its technical and aesthetic importance, and in many cases, the author's personal response to the film.

For a full list of titles in the series, please visit
https://www.bloomsbury.com/uk/series/bfi-film-classics/

T0371884

# All the President's Men

Christian Keathley
and Robert B. Ray

THE BRITISH FILM INSTITUTE
Bloomsbury Publishing Plc
50 Bedford Square, London, WC1B 3DP, UK
1385 Broadway, New York, NY 10018, USA
29 Earlsfort Terrace, Dublin 2, Ireland

BLOOMSBURY is a trademark of Bloomsbury Publishing Plc

First published in Great Britain 2023 by Bloomsbury on behalf of the
British Film Institute
21 Stephen Street, London W1T 1LN
www.bfi.org.uk

The BFI is the lead organisation for film in the UK and the distributor of Lottery funds for film.
Our mission is to ensure that film is central to our cultural life, in particular by supporting and
nurturing the next generation of filmmakers and audiences. We serve a public role which covers
the cultural, creative and economic aspects of film in the UK.

Cover artwork: © gray318
Series cover design: Louise Dugdale
Series text design: Ketchup/SE14
Images from *All the President's Men* (Alan J. Pakula, 1976), © Warner Bros./Wildwood Enterprises;
*The Maltese Falcon* (John Huston, 1941), © Warner Bros.; *La Règle du jeu* (Jean Renoir, 1939), Nouvelle
Édition Française

A catalogue record for this book is available from the British Library.

A catalog record for this book is available from the Library of Congress.

ISBN:    PB:    978-1-8390-2404-7
        ePDF:   978-1-8390-2406-1
        ePUB:   978-1-8390-2405-4

Produced for Bloomsbury Publishing Plc by Sophie Contento
Printed and bound in India

# Contents

Acknowledgments 6

*All the President's Men* 7

Chronology of Events Portrayed in
*All the President's Men* 104

Credits 109

Bibliography 111

## Acknowledgments

We want especially to recognise our debt to Craig Cieslikowski. He offered his notes on *All the President's Men*, which provided us with most of this book's first sentence. He also called our attention to such details as the mysterious 'Pete Teller', Woodward's crutch and Hoffman's manoeuvring in the Bookkeeper's doorway. Craig's remarks on the film prompted us to undertake our own similar detective work. We are grateful to him.

We also want to thank Bloomsbury's Rebecca Barden, who approved this book, and Sophie Contento, who saw it through to publication.

James Naremore encouraged us to write about *All the President's Men*, and a one-semester research leave, granted by the University of Florida's English Department Chair Sid Dobrin, enabled us to complete it.

## All the President's Men

It is as if a snapshot of a scene had been taken, but only a few scattered details of it were to be seen: here a hand, there a bit of a face, or a hat – the rest is dark. And now it is as if we knew quite certainly what the whole picture represented. As if I could read the darkness.

Ludwig Wittgenstein,
*Philosophical Investigations* (Section 635) (1953)

*All the President's Men* is a film about asking questions, taking notes and making connections. Like the scandal it treats, it is in many ways a secretive work, often concealing an intricately purposeful design to hide in plain sight, under the guise of a commercial picture, its status as what Alan J. Pakula's assistant called 'almost an art movie' (Gaynor 2016). This book will regard *All the President's Men* as an instruction manual for writing about it: asking questions and taking notes and making connections to uncover its ways of working. Its method will imitate that of the reporters who investigated the Watergate story, accumulating inferences incrementally and indirectly, triggered by details whose initial significance often seems just out of reach. Christopher Ricks once suggested that 'criticism is the art of noticing things that the rest of us may well not have noticed for ourselves and might never have noticed. … it must neither state nor neglect the obvious' (Burrow 2021). Such noticing is what critics, detectives and investigative reporters have in common.

### Two origins
*All the President's Men* premiered at Washington's Kennedy Center on 4 April 1976 and became the sixth most popular movie of that year. Behind it lay two events that decisively affected how the film was made.

The first event occurred in the early hours of 17 June 1972: the arrest of the five men, equipped with bugging devices, who had broken into the Democratic National Committee's offices in the Watergate Office Building. The subsequent investigation and cover-up of this burglary came to be known as The Watergate Scandal, which dominated the news for the next two years. *ATPM*, in other words, derives not only from *Washington Post* reporters Bob Woodward and Carl Bernstein's account of that scandal, but also from a real historical event that had happened just four years before and whose outcome, the resignation of President Richard M. Nixon, had been one of the biggest stories in US history.

Movies based on real events, of course, are common. *The Life of Emile Zola* (1937), for example, dramatises the novelist's role in vindicating Alfred Dreyfus, a French army captain falsely convicted of espionage. But *L'Affaire Dreyfus*, lasting for eight years and as famous in France as Watergate became in the US, had taken place more than thirty years before the Warner Bros. movie – and in a foreign country to boot. Few Americans in the late 1930s would have been familiar with its twists and turns, or even with the story's basic outline.

Watergate, however, was more immediate. When Robert Redford first proposed *All the President's Men* to the studio where he had a production deal (Warner Bros. again), he met with a crucial objection: every potential viewer already knew how this story turned out. That objection signalled Warners' intention for the film. Instead of the Redford-proposed black-and-white documentary-style movie with unknown actors (Brown 2005: 150), Warners wanted what the film's poster would call 'The most devastating detective story of this century'. But how do you make a detective story out of a case whose solution everybody knows? The film-makers' answer to that question holds the key to the movie.

The second event occurred in October 1972, when Redford discovered a profile about Woodward and Bernstein, the names attached to the Watergate stories he had followed since the scandal's beginning (Brown 2005: 150). In July 1972, just weeks after the break-in, Woodward had undertaken a rare promotional tour for *The Candidate*, a movie he had co-written about an idealist running for the US Senate. The promotion, an imitation whistle-stop train trip from Jacksonville to Miami, included over forty reporters, whose indifference to the Watergate story shocked Redford. It also quickened his attention to the *Post* accounts. Until October, however, Woodward and Bernstein had been only names. The profile made them distinct characters: Bernstein, the twenty-eight-year-old Jewish Democrat, a college drop-out with twelve years of journalism experience; Woodward, the twenty-nine-year-old WASP Republican, a Yale alumnus with only nine months at *The Post*. Bernstein was volatile, intuitive and undisciplined. Woodward was calm, dogged and cautious. Butch Cassidy and the Sundance Kid? Redford saw the possibilities. The idea of a *paired opposition* would determine the organising formal strategy developed by the film-making team.

## Who's in control?

The history of the cinema involves a recurring debate about the proper site of control over the film-making process. During the cottage industry phase, individuals like D. W. Griffith and Erich von Stroheim operated as laws unto themselves, working simultaneously as producer, writer, director, editor and (in von Stroheim's case) star of their own movies. As the Hollywood studios consolidated in the 1920s, control moved upwards to the central producer, responsible for every stage of production. Pioneered by MGM's Irving Thalberg, this model persisted into the 1950s, when it faced two challenges: (1) the increasing power of stars (e.g. James Stewart, Burt Lancaster and John Wayne) who created their own film-making units; and (2) the revolt of the French New Wave's auteur policy, which insisted on the director's ultimate authority. Following the New Wave's international success, auteurism became the new dispensation, with directors becoming their own brands. Arthur Penn, Stanley Kubrick,

Sam Peckinpah, Francis Ford Coppola, Steven Spielberg and Martin Scorsese regained the control the cottage industry men had lost to the studio system. With film-making decisions now ceded to directors, the increasingly conglomerate-owned studios even tolerated the inevitable self-indulgent casualties like *Apocalypse Now* (1979) or *Heaven's Gate* (1980).

One of the most interesting things about *All the President's Men* is that it does not fit this new auteurist model. Its director, Alan J. Pakula, had begun as a producer (most famously on *To Kill a Mockingbird* [1962]), and despite the success of *Klute* (1971), his adaptable style never won auteur critics' attention. Though *Klute*, *The Parallax View* (1974) and *ATPM* are often grouped together as Pakula's 'paranoia trilogy', they have little in common, stylistically or thematically, with the films he directed before or after. *All the President's Men* (billed as 'A Robert Redford–Alan J. Pakula Film') resembles a studio-era picture, the result of the active collaboration of a creative producer (Redford), multiple scriptwriters (William Goldman, Pakula and Redford), a skilful director (Pakula), major stars (Redford and Dustin Hoffman), a distinctive cameraman (Gordon Willis), imaginative art directors (George Jenkins and George Gaines) and a team of ingenious sound designers. Nominated for seven Academy Awards (picture, director, supporting actor and actress, screenplay, sound and art direction), the movie won four: Jason Robards, Jr for supporting actor; Goldman for screenplay; Arthur Piantadosi, Les Fresholtz, Dick Alexander and Jim Webb for sound; and Jenkins and Gaines for art direction/set decoration. The Best Picture Oscar went to *Rocky*, the year's box-office number one.

Redford had initiated the production, not only buying the rights to Woodward and Bernstein's book, but also prompting them to shift their original focus on the story's events to their own roles in investigating them. (Told about that suggestion, Woodward and Bernstein's Simon & Schuster editor concurred: 'I like Redford's idea better' [Brown 2005: 152]). Redford hired, or approved the hiring of, Pakula, Hoffman and Robards, who would play *Post* editor Ben Bradlee. By all accounts, however, once shooting began, Redford relinquished control, deferring to Pakula and Willis. 'Once you're on the set,' Redford acknowledged, 'there can be only one captain, the director. And I expected conflict' (Hirshberg 1976: 57). Pakula, after all, had not been Redford's first choice. He had approached Hal Ashby, Elia Kazan, Arthur Penn, Joseph Mankiewicz and John Badham before, at the last minute, Pakula became available (Boorstin 2016; Hirshberg 1976: 98).

## Casting I

Jean Renoir once advised François Truffaut that casting was the most important part of film-making; if you get it wrong, Renoir cautioned, nothing works. The most important casting decision for *All the President's Men* occurred when, having rejected Redford's initial proposal to use unknown actors, Warner Bros. insisted that he star in the film himself. Pakula agreed. With Redford clinging to the idea of a quasi-documentary – and planning to dye his hair to disappear into the Woodward role – Pakula argued, as his assistant Jon Boorstin remembers, that 'the plot was so complicated that they couldn't afford to waste time on character exposition. ... he quoted Hitchcock's dictum that casting a star saves twenty minutes of character development' since the audience already 'knows' the star (Boorstin 1995: 156).

With Redford set as Woodward, Warners pointed out that the film would need another star to play Bernstein. After Redford's brief consideration of Al Pacino, Dustin Hoffman became the choice, but Redford delayed offering him the part, telephoning him just six months before the start of shooting. Hoffman, who had considered buying the book's rights himself, quickly accepted: 'I thought you'd never ask' (Hirshberg 1976: 77). *ATPM* had its two leads. 'Between them,' Elizabeth Kraft notes, 'they defined American male stardom ... in their opposite looks, roles, and performance styles' (Kraft 2008: 31).

Redford and Hoffman were born in the same city (Los Angeles) in the same year (1937). Both spent most of their twenties in New York, working in theatre and television. Despite these biographical coincidences, *All the President's Men* is the only movie in which they appeared together. The classical era's studio system, with its exclusive contracts and infrequent loan-outs, had made that phenomenon common: MGM's Clark Gable, for example, never shared a film with Warner Bros.' Humphrey Bogart or RKO's Cary Grant. But in the post-studio world, when movie stars had acquired the freedom to do what they liked, Redford's and Hoffman's diverging choices tell us something about how they thought of themselves.

Redford had more stage success. While Hoffman appeared only off-Broadway and in regional theatre, Redford managed five Broadway parts, the first as a replacement in *Tall Story* (1959), co-written by Russell Crouse, whose daughter Lindsay would make her film debut in *ATPM*. After two flops, he starred in *Barefoot in the Park* (1963), the play that made Neil Simon famous. But his movie career began slowly: a repeat of *Tall Story* (1960); as a bisexual, unhappily married to Natalie Wood in *Inside Daisy Clover* (1965); as the rabbit, the mostly non-speaking escaped (innocent) convict Bubber Reeves, pursued by Marlon Brando and Jane Fonda in *The Chase* (1966); with Fonda again, reprising *Barefoot in the Park* (1967). And then came the enormous hit *Butch Cassidy and the Sundance Kid* (1969), opposite his ideal co-star Paul Newman. The film established the image that he would both exploit and flee: he was already thirty-two, but looked younger, conveying a boyish artlessness that would mark his subsequent roles. (During the events portrayed in *ATPM*, for example, Bob Woodward was a decade younger than the man who would play him.)

Redford, however, was artistically ambitious and eager to escape, at least occasionally, from audience expectations. Remarkably good-looking, even by movie standards, he may have been the first major male star who was blond. (Two earlier possibilities, Alan Ladd and James Dean, were never quite major stars.) Unlike his idiosyncratic predecessors, Redford was classically handsome, and his fans tended to talk about his appearance rather than his acting. (With Hoffman, it was the reverse.) Like a gifted comedian who regards tragedy as 'more serious', or the beautiful woman who wants respect for her brains, Redford appeared to hoard his sunburst smile, releasing it only intermittently for movies like *The Sting* (1973) and *The Natural* (1984), the latter showing off his baseball prowess. His taste was fundamentally middlebrow, encouraging him to choose earnest projects like *The Way We Were* (1973), *Ordinary People* (for which he won the Best Director Oscar in 1980), *Brubaker* (1980) and *A River Runs Through It* (which he directed in 1992). But *ATPM* – which Redford bought, produced, co-wrote, starred in and helped edit – proves that he has never been just another pretty face. The resulting movie was a miracle, saved from its potential deadly seriousness by the film-making team's extraordinary imagination.

After a busy, but little seen, theatrical career, Hoffman hit with his second movie, *The Graduate* (1967). His performance as Benjamin – the dazed college graduate with a deer-in-the-headlights expression – looked like simple personification. But Hoffman was almost thirty and an alumnus of The Actors Studio, home of the Method; he was anything but guileless, and Benjamin amounted to the first of his serial disguises. The Academy, always more impressed by biographical impersonation than autobiographical personification, recognised the achievement and nominated Hoffman for the Best Actor Oscar. In his next released picture, *Midnight Cowboy* (1969), he intensified the camouflage, concealing his own appearance in the make-up, costuming, limp and accent that transformed him into Ratso Rizzo. Presto: his second Oscar nomination. Ultimately, he would earn seven, winning twice: for *Kramer vs. Kramer* (1979) and *Rain Man* (1988). Of the seven, *Tootsie* (1982), where he plays an out-of-work actor who gets work by disguising himself as a woman, is the most autobiographical, amounting to an allegory of Hoffman's own career in pictures like *Little Big Man* (1970) and *Papillon* (1973).

Hoffman's choices indicated that his idea of acting derived from the theatre. Playing a part involved impersonation and using all the tricks of the trade to work himself into a character remote from himself. Perhaps aware that, unlike Redford, he could not rely on his looks (Robert Duvall, a former roommate, once described him as 'Barbra Streisand in drag'), he was rarely content simply to let himself be observed by the camera. On a set, he grew increasingly fussy, asking for more rehearsals, proposing additional bits of business. In *ATPM*, Pakula takes advantage of these tendencies by opposing Hoffman's nervous fluttering to the Bookkeeper's anxious stillness and Woodward's dogged calm. Hoffman has never been better.

While making *ATPM*, Redford and Hoffman unconsciously reprised the dynamic between the casually self-confident Bing Crosby, always happy with a single take, and the never-satisfied perfectionist Fred Astaire, who always wanted one more. Bringing Hoffman on board set up a contrast between Redford's classic Hollywood style and Hoffman's Method acting. As James Naremore (1988) has noted, a star can underplay compared to supporting actors, content to let his or her familiar appearance and behaviour simply be recorded by the camera. Jon Boorstin distils that point into a dictum: 'a star is someone you can watch doing nothing'

(Boorstin 1995: 71). Redford's performance in *ATPM* is straightforward; Hoffman's is more mannered, appropriate to someone fundamentally a character actor. Pakula quickly sensed the difference:

Bob is intuitive and bright and makes quick, bold decisions which are frequently correct. Then he gets impatient. Dustin is quite different. Dustin's creative rhythm is slower. No matter how well he does a scene, he always wants to try one more. Or one more rehearsal. ... Bob's acting explodes from a certain spontaneous and emotional concentration, and this can be lost through repeated retakes. (Hirshberg 1976: 104)

The Academy has rarely rewarded performers like Redford, who received his only Best Actor nomination for *The Sting*, a cleverly commercial caper movie. Like many other unrecognised great stars – William Powell, John Wayne, Cary Grant – Redford often seemed to be simply playing himself, his skill at appearing natural before the camera perceived as mere effortlessness. We should not, however, underestimate Redford's *ATPM* performance, at its most effective during his calls to potential sources. Look, for example, at 14:10, when Woodward telephones the White House and asks for Howard Hunt. The receptionist's matter-of-fact reply – 'Mr Hunt isn't here just now' – amounts to a shocking gold-strike. In close-up, Redford responds with only the slightest gesture of pleased surprise, a tiny flicker around the eyes and mouth.

The moment demonstrates what distinguishes the movies from the stage, where such a minimal gesture would go unremarked. Having come from the theatre, James Stewart recalled having to learn this lesson from Margaret Sullavan, who kept telling him, 'Less, less.' Redford seems instinctively to have understood this dictum, employing it masterfully in his greatest moment as an actor, the six-minute shot of him on the phone with Kenneth Dahlberg and Clark MacGregor. With MacGregor on the line at 51:25 Woodward gets a return call from Dahlberg, who has just hung up on him.

Asking MacGregor to hold, Redford distils his excitement into
raising his two forefingers to his closed eyes, while he cradles the
phone against his shoulder.

At the end of Dahlberg's riveting conversation, filled with
crucial revelations, Redford (perhaps improvising around a mistake)
says, 'Mr MacGregor ... Mr Dahlberg', while raising his left hand to
his forehead and his right hand to the side of his face. Nothing more.
Redford accomplished this exceptionally demanding scene on the
second take.

During the movie's shooting, the Redford–Hoffman contrast
surfaced in other ways. Boorstin remembers that while Hoffman
would show up on time, Redford would come late. While Redford

was quickly ready for a take, Hoffman 'had to try things until he found his scene. A coincidence perhaps, but … Hoffman would improvise and experiment and prepare for however long that Redford had been late' (Boorstin 2016).

How did Hoffman's casting affect the movie? What does an actor 'mean'? Performers aren't like words, whose definitions we can look up in a dictionary. The semioticians' commutation test, however, provides one way of getting at what an actor conveys: as a thought experiment, try different people in the same role and imagine how the film would change. In 1976, only a few actors seemed possible replacements for Hoffman. Richard Dreyfuss, Richard Benjamin and Elliott Gould are, like Carl Bernstein, Jewish, but *ATPM* needed a star as big as Redford to establish the Woodward–Bernstein equal partnership, and casting any of these three would have thrown the movie off balance. Benjamin (6 ft 2 in.) and Gould (6 ft 3 in.) are also too tall to match up with Redford, whose height (slightly less than 5 ft 10 in.) resembles Woodward's. At 5 ft 6 in., Hoffman made a good fit for Bernstein (5 ft 8 in.), while more importantly providing a visually appealing Mutt-and-Jeff pairing with Redford. Dreyfuss (5 ft 5 in.) seems a closer fit than the others, but he never achieved the star presence of Hoffman.

Perhaps the most intriguing possibility for the Bernstein part would have been Redford's first idea, Al Pacino (5 ft 7 in.). Although not Jewish, his street-smart urban persona would have suited the Bernstein role, and the two enormously successful *Godfather* films (1972 and 1974) had made him a star the equal of Redford. But those movies would also have presented a problem. Character actors like Hoffman impersonate; stars like Redford personify. While Hoffman had always proved able to shed previous roles, making his audience forget Ratso Rizzo (*Midnight Cowboy*), Jack Crabb (*Little Big Man*) and Louis Dega (*Papillon*), Pacino had become so memorable as the cold, guarded, calculating Michael Corleone that he would have made Bernstein (who, in reality, was volatile and unreserved) seem distractingly sinister.

Could any actor other than Redford have played Bob Woodward? Some obvious choices like Paul Newman and Robert Duvall were too old, and Gene Hackman *looked* too old. Jack Nicholson was too manic and Robert De Niro (whom Redford considered for both roles) too intimidating to play a reporter like Woodward, who used a polite, ingratiating manner to get people to reveal things they had carefully kept hidden.

## Casting II: the lock

For a movie that Warner Bros. advertised as a detective story, *ATPM* does something uniquely risky: it keeps its villains off screen. While actors play the *Post* reporters and their sources (including Deep Throat), only Donald Segretti, a minor accomplice in the scandal, gets similar treatment. But a few of the actual antagonists do appear on the television screens scattered around the *Post*'s office: President Nixon; Speaker of the House Gerald Ford; Attorney General Richard Kleindienst; Vice President Spiro Agnew; Press Secretary Ronald Ziegler. *ATPM* also provides a newspaper front page with a photograph of former Attorney General John Mitchell and the audio of an interview with Nixon's Campaign Manager, Clark MacGregor.

In *S/Z*, Roland Barthes pointed to Balzac's similar willingness to introduce historical figures – Napoleon, Diderot, Rousseau – into a fictional world. Their function, Barthes argued, depends precisely on their being seen only '*in passing*', for if these people were to assume their '*real* importance', they would overwhelm the story and 'paradoxically, make it less real'. Instead, their modest appearances function, Barthes proposed, 'like a lock between two levels of water, [equalising] novel and history' (Barthes 1974: 101–2). Thus, in *ATPM*, the brief television images of Nixon's men lift the actors' performances to the villains' historical level, encouraging us to forget that 'Woodward' and 'Bernstein' are Robert Redford and Dustin Hoffman. To see this effect work in the opposite direction, you only have to look at Charles Ferguson's *Watergate* (2018), where using actors to play Nixon, Haldeman and Ehrlichman undercuts the documentary, making it seem as if the Watergate events never happened – except in a fictional world.

## Casting III: documentary and fiction – the case of the tourist photographer and the curious child

A simple five-shot sequence:

Shot 1: long shot of a line of tourists waiting on a pavement to visit the White House. All are looking straight ahead except for two people. One is a man wearing sunglasses, an open-necked white dress shirt and light grey slacks. He looks across the street, holding a camera. The other is a little girl near the front of the line. She faces the street, seeming to look across it. Bernstein's voice becomes audible: 'So come on, what's going on with you guys at the FBI? I've been trying to get you for weeks.'

Shot 2 [next page]: long shot of Bernstein and his FBI informant, Joe (Jess Osuna), coming around a corner, with the tourist line just visible through the traffic, on the other side of the street. Bernstein continues: 'Your secretary says you're not in. Last night I called you, and you said you couldn't talk, and this morning, as soon as our Mitchell story hits the stands, you call and say you gotta see me right away. Why?'

Shot 3 [below]: medium shot of Bernstein and Joe walking from right to left. Joe explains: 'Because you guys have been causing big trouble at the Bureau.' Bernstein: 'Why?' Joe: 'Our reports are showing up in your paper almost verbatim. I mean you've really been on the mark. [The camera closes in on them, as Joe stops and sticks his finger in Bernstein's chest.] Except for Mitchell. Now we didn't have that. [Bernstein smiles smugly. They resume walking.] That he controlled the fund.' Bernstein: 'Right.' Joe: 'Our agents have been busting ass, but we're going back now to see if we've missed anything.' Joe bends over to tie his left shoe.

Bernstein: 'But, Joe, what I don't understand is that all the people who might know details [Bernstein looks back over his

shoulder] of the bugging operations the FBI hasn't even talked to. And why have you conducted your interviews with CREEP personnel at CREEP headquarters instead of at their homes where they might be freer to talk?' [Bernstein looks behind him.] Joe: 'I do what I'm told. I followed my orders. Period.' [Joe looks in the direction of the street. Bernstein looks in the same direction.]

Shot 4: tourist line waiting on the pavement, as in Shot 1. The white-shirted man is now taking a photograph of something across the street, in the direction established as that of Bernstein and Joe. Two other men are also taking photographs, but not in Bernstein and Joe's direction. Shot 1's curious child is no longer looking across the street.

Shot 5: cut back to the two shot of Bernstein and Joe, who now bends over to tie his right shoe. Bernstein: 'What orders?' [The scene ends.]

Here are some possibilities:

1. The film-makers hire extras to portray tourists waiting in a pavement line to visit the White House. They instruct one of the extras to dress like an off-duty CIA agent and point his camera across the street. They ask another extra, a little girl, to face the street and look towards it.
2. The film-makers stage the scene to incorporate a line of ordinary tourists, two of whom notice the camera across the street. One photographs Hoffman and Osuna. The other, a little girl, also stares before losing interest.
3. The film-makers hire one man to embed himself in a line of regular tourists and pretend to take photographs of something happening across the street.

As shot, the sequence makes it impossible to tell which of these possibilities is in play. The first, of course, would amount to standard, fully controlled film-making. The second would use eyeline matches to make an unplanned event (the photographer's aim) appear to affect behaviour in the fictional world (Joe's and Bernstein's staged, furtive glances). The third would acknowledge that the scene would perhaps seem more real if only one of the 'tourists' is a plant. There are differences, however. The extras in the first possibility would see the film-making crew and have been told that Hoffman is playing Carl Bernstein. In the second possibility, the photographer would recognise Dustin Hoffman but not Carl Bernstein. (Presumably, he would not recognise Jess Osuna.) In other words, *he would not see the fiction*. In the third possibility, only the one hired extra would see it.

The scene's effect results from the cinema's inevitable mixture of documentary and fiction, a function of the camera's indifference to the distinction between them. V. F. Perkins described this factor:

> The camera does not discriminate between real events (which would have taken place even if it had not been on the spot to record them) and action created specifically in order to be recorded. In this respect, the movie simply extends the ambiguity present in any credible image; so long as it looks correct we have no way of telling whether a picture portrays an actual or an imagined subject. (Perkins 1993: 68)

The ambiguity was present from the movies' beginnings. As Dai Vaughan showed, the amalgam of documentary and fiction makes ambiguous even the simplest of films like Lumière's 40-second *L'Arroseur arrosé* (1895): (a) was the joke entirely staged? (b) was only an uninformed gardener surprised? (c) did the boy and the gardener surprise Lumière? (d) did the gardener's retaliation surprise the boy?, etc. (Vaughan 1999: 6–7). More than most films, *ATPM* depends on this mixture: the location shooting, the nearly exact replica of the *Post*'s newsroom, and, above all, the story's basis in actual events all contribute to the realistic urgency that conventional studio-bound filming would have diluted. The tourist sequence also demonstrates how movie stars sit precisely at the juncture of fiction and documentary. Godard once remarked that *À bout de souffle/ Breathless* (1959) was, at the very least, a documentary about

Jean-Paul Belmondo and Jean Seberg, and all movies work that way. If you want, for example, to see what Jean Harlow looked like only three days after her husband Paul Bern was found dead from an apparent, but unconfirmed, suicide, you only have to look at a scene from *Red Dust* (1932), to whose shooting she had returned, her puffy features partially concealed by a soft-focus lens.

Movie stars provide a perfect example of Wittgenstein's duck-rabbit, the ambiguous gestalt image with two aspects. Having begun to watch *ATPM*, at what point does a viewer stop seeing Robert Redford and only see 'Bob Woodward'? Does Redford ever disappear entirely? Does 'Woodward' ever recede? What would prompt either perceptual shift? Why do we tend to refer to a movie's characters by their stars' names ('and then Redford picked up the telephone, and Hoffman kept typing')? Are films that encourage us to see the character rather than the star 'better' than those that do the reverse? Does saying 'yes' to that question amount to a prejudice against commercial cinema? Is Paul Muni a better film actor than John Wayne? What factors make our perception of Redford, as opposed to his character, more persistent than our perception of Hoffman? Does one definition of movie stardom depend on that persistence?

### The problem of the detective story whose ending everyone knows – the Hemingway solution

The Warners executives who worried that the Watergate scandal's outcome was already common knowledge had a legitimate concern. Why read *The Murder of Roger Ackroyd* if you know the killer from the start? Redford had advised Woodward and Bernstein to make the book *their* story. Following that advice, *ATPM*'s film-makers would make a crucial decision: the movie would *simulate the reporters' experience* of perplexity, confusion and illegibility. 'We have all these pieces,' Woodward tells Deep Throat; 'we just can't seem to figure out what the puzzle is supposed to look like.' The viewer would be put through the same bewilderment.

In effect, Redford and Pakula had adopted the storytelling model described by Ernest Hemingway:

I have tried to eliminate everything unnecessary to conveying experience to the reader so that after he or she has read something it will become a part of his or her experience and seem actually to have happened. This is very hard to do and I have worked at it very hard. (Brooks 1966: 236)

For *ATPM*, this effect would require the film-makers to reproduce the borderline illegibility experienced by Woodward and Bernstein. *The movie could not be too clear*. When Gilbert Ryle's *The Concept of Mind* (1949) appeared, Wittgenstein objected that the way in which Ryle treated philosophical problems made them 'lose their magic' (Mendieta 2005: 77). The film-makers engaged in *ATPM* had to maintain a delicate balance: Woodward and Bernstein's discoveries had to cohere, but they could not cohere so readily or neatly that the mysteries behind them, or the investigations of them, would 'lose their magic'.

The difficulty is at least as old as the novel. With what E. M. Forster called its clues and 'chains of cause and effect', plot is fundamentally unrealistic, its patterns misrepresentative of everyday life, described in *A Passage to India* (1924) as often 'so dull that there is nothing to be said about it'. A commercial film, however, cannot risk boring its audience, even with the purpose of getting closer to the way things really are. It has to tell a story that makes its viewers want to know what happens next. The problem posed by the Watergate scandal is that most people already knew.

The film-makers' solution, in Hemingway's terms, was to provide the equivalent of the reporters' experience – the confusion, the impasses, the set-backs, the need to keep starting over – so that the viewer will share it. If this approach seems obvious, one again has only to compare *ATPM* to Charles Ferguson's 261-minute *Watergate*, a step-by-step procession of logical developments that never allows the audience to experience the sensation described by Woodward and

Bernstein – the feeling of being lost. *ATPM* would achieve its quality of illegibility in two ways – through scripting and *mise en scène*.

## Script vs. movie – omissions and contradictions, causal links and missing contexts

Redford's first choice for converting *ATPM* into a movie was William Goldman, who had previously written three of the actor's films: the enormously successful *Butch Cassidy and the Sundance Kid*, *The Hot Rock* (1972) and *The Great Waldo Pepper* (1975). Having just finished adapting his own novel *Marathon Man* (1974) for a 1976 Dustin Hoffman picture, Goldman threw himself into this new job, travelling to Washington to meet with Woodward and Bernstein and learn the ways of the *Post*'s newsroom. Always a fast writer, Goldman completed a first draft in six weeks (Hirshberg 1976: 47–8). He knew detective stories, having turned Ross Macdonald's *The Moving Target* (1949) into Paul Newman's *Harper* (1966). Goldman also understood the basic problem:

The audience that views the film will, in a sense, be smarter than the heroes. The audience knows Nixon was involved and that there was a cover-up. ... But Woodward and Bernstein didn't know it at the time. ... you have to keep the picture interesting, surprising without playing games. (Hirshberg 1976: 90–1)

Goldman had not, however, recognised the advantages of Hemingway's method, which would make the viewer *experience* Woodward and Bernstein's confusion. What he came up with Redford described as 'slick, very clever and jokey' (Hirshberg 1976: 91). 'It was written very quickly, and it went for comedy. It trivialized not only the event but journalism' (Brown 2005: 153). Woodward had a similar response: 'It's not that it was bad, it's that it missed; it could have been much better' (Hirshberg 1976: 91). Pakula agreed: 'I don't want to make *Butch Woodward and the Sundance Bernstein*, you know' (Brown 2005: 155).

But for all of his script's faults, Goldman had made a vital contribution: he had seen where to end the movie. Woodward and Bernstein's book concluded with the March 1974 grand jury indictment of Nixon's men – Haldeman, Ehrlichman, Colson and Mitchell. Goldman would 'throw away the last half of the book' and set the film's final scene in January 1973, immediately after the reporters' biggest blunder, their failure to confirm that Hugh Sloan had been asked by the grand jury about Haldeman's involvement (Brown 2005: 153). Redford recognised Goldman's contribution:

what Bill Goldman had done in that first draft almost instinctively was come up with a better structure than anyone had thought possible. ...
It was the key to telling the story in terms of the cinema – which is a vastly different medium than a book. We had the key now. The words would follow.
(Hirshberg 1976: 91)

The first words led down a blind alley. Carl Bernstein and his girlfriend Nora Ephron produced their own screenplay, making Bernstein a romantic hero, while managing to alienate both Woodward and Goldman. Redford quickly rejected this script, telling Bernstein, 'Carl, Errol Flynn is dead' (Brown 2005: 154). Instead, Redford and Pakula decided to take on the job themselves, moving into a hotel to rewrite the screenplay over the course of a month. And then, when the filming began, interesting things happened.

In classical cinema, the process from scripting to final cut typically involves revising for purposes of greater narrative clarity and efficiency. But with *All the President's Men*, the changes at these successive stages – adapting the book into a script, revising the script, filming and editing – often served to obscure what was originally clear. Conventional motion picture narrative proceeds by causal links that lead us from one scene to the next, clarifying plot information as well as character actions and goals. But throughout *All the President's Men*, such causal links are routinely omitted or obscured.

An example: Early in the film, when Woodward visits the courthouse to report on the Watergate burglars' arraignment, he asks a group of men standing in the lobby who among them is the public defender of record, only to be told that the burglars had arranged for their own legal representation.

WOODWARD    You know the name of the counsel?
MAN         I don't know. Some country club type.

From here, we cut to a medium shot of the lawyer, Markham, seated in the courtroom gallery, dressed neatly in a crisp grey-blue three-piece suit. After a few moments, Woodward sits down behind him. The following shot of the courtroom shows a variety of lawyers, their clients and spectators. We then return to the previous shot of Markham and Woodward, who waits several seconds before leaning forward to ask the man's name and whether he is there in connection with the Watergate burglary. *But how did Woodward know this was the man to approach?*

The script had made it clear. At the conclusion of the scene in the courthouse lobby, Woodward asks a man (whom the script identifies as the Clerk), 'What's the counsel's name?' – but we would cut to the next scene before he replies. Then, as the script had it:

INT. THE COURTROOM – DAY
Muggers, pimps, hookers, their families and friends.

INT. THE AUDIENCE – DAY
One man stands out – MARKHAM. He is extremely well-dressed and obviously successful. Beside him sits another smaller man, who is unshaven and squints. Woodward moves in, sits alongside.

WOODWARD    Mr Markham? Bob Woodward, I'm from *The Post*.

The script version of the scene emphasises the causal link. We can infer that Woodward has been told the lawyer's name (he says it when he sits down behind him), and that he has been able to identify the lawyer because he looks conspicuously different from the other people in the courtroom. The script clearly indicates an establishing shot of the courtroom filled with people who are definitely not the 'country club type', and this shot is designated to appear *before* Woodward sits down with Markham. The script's imagined ordering of shots – establishing shot of the courtroom, followed by a closer shot of Markham, perhaps prompted by Woodward's glance – would have not only followed découpage norms, but would have also allowed us to understand how Woodward was able to pick the lawyer out of the crowd.

In the film scene, by contrast, the man that Woodward questions states that he does not know the lawyer's name. From the line, 'Some country club type', we cut to the medium shot of Markham, with Woodward then sitting down behind him, and only then do we get the wider shot of the courtroom. But even here, the shot does not match the script's description. It registers simply as a wide shot of a courtroom, half-filled with a variety of people (a number of whom wear suits, like Markham). Thus, in the film version of the scene, how Woodward has been able to identify the man is left for us to guess.

Another example: After Bernstein's conversation with the White House Librarian, the reporters head to the Library of Congress to find evidence that Howard Hunt had been requesting books on Senator Edward Kennedy. There follows a two-minute, five-second sequence in which they try unsuccessfully to get proof. As they leave the building, frustrated, Woodward – in long shot and with his back to the camera – suddenly announces, 'Hey, wait a minute. I met a White House aide once at a social occasion. He might confirm.' From here we cut to Woodward and Bernstein back in the *Post* newsroom working on the story. The intervening scene, in which they must have followed up this scene, has been left out – even though the script had included a subsequent scene of Woodward telephoning the source from a payphone, and then sharing confirmation with the waiting Bernstein. The omission of this scene of their success, and the inclusion only of scenes of their failure, marks a strange causal rupture in the film's narrative continuity.

The film also suppresses explanatory contexts. One of the movie's key plot points involves the reporters' discovery that the Deputy Director of White House Communications, Ken Clawson, was responsible for writing the 'Canuck letter' – which, as Bernstein repeatedly states, claimed that Democratic candidate Edmund Muskie had 'slurred the Canadians'. In spite of its apparent importance in the film, no context for this letter is provided. As a result, viewers are left to ask themselves: *What exactly was this letter? Where did it appear? Why would such a letter sink a candidate's campaign?*

The details are these: Early in the 1972 primary campaign, someone wrote a letter to the Manchester (NH) *Union Leader*, stating that, during a campaign stop in Florida, an aide to Muskie had made an offensive remark comparing Blacks to Canucks (French Canadians) living in New England. The letter further claimed that, when asked what the aide meant, Muskie laughed and said, 'Come to New England and see.' Publication of the letter prompted Muskie to hold a press conference just three days before the New Hampshire primary and denounce it as fake. In this speech, Muskie allegedly broke down several times – though his 'tears' may have been snowflakes melting on his face – and people took to calling it 'the crying speech'. Although Muskie had been polling well, his showing in the first Democratic primary in New Hampshire was disappointing. Many believe that the crying speech made him appear emotionally unstable, and this conclusion led to his downfall in the primaries.

In their notes to Redford after viewing an early screening, Woodward and Bernstein complained, 'The reference to the Canuck letter is very obscure. The letter is important because it made Muskie look like a racist (re French Canadians in N. H.) and led him into a blunder (crying in public) that destroyed him in NH' (Bernstein and Woodward 1975). While it might be argued that some viewers in

1976 would have recalled the details of this event, Hollywood rarely relies on such familiarity. Indeed, film adaptations in Hollywood routinely proceed as if no potential viewer had ever read the book or knew the story.

Yet another important contextual element is missing from this sequence about the Canuck letter. When Clawson telephones Ben Bradlee in his office, Ben props his feet up on his desk and greets him happily: 'Hey, Ken! What's up, kid?' What explains this casual tone of interaction between a newspaperman and a White House official? In fact, before taking a job at the White House, Ken Clawson had been a reporter at *The Washington Post*. This unmentioned history would also have helped to explain his acquaintance with *Post* reporter Sally Aiken (in the script identified as Marilyn Berger), the colleague who shares the crucial information about the letter's authorship with Woodward and Bernstein, but the movie omits it.

To highlight here the ways in which the processes of scripting and filming – at the most basic informational plot level – moved from clarity to near illegibility, we can turn to a series of scenes in which the reporters investigate CREEP's (Committee to Re-elect the President) secret cash fund.

In the first scene, Bernstein meets with the CREEP Bookkeeper (Jane Alexander), who tells him that fifteen people received payments from the secret cash fund, and that about five people (she doesn't know who) had power to disburse money. When they return to discussing the men who got money (the fifteen), they emphasise just three, and these only by their initials: L, P and M. In the following scene of the two reporters in Woodward's apartment, their conversation focuses on who L, P and M might be. But then, in a subsequent scene with Hugh Sloan, the whole question of *who got money* – L, P and M (Liddy, Porter and Magruder) – has been dropped and replaced with a focus on *those in control of disbursing money* from the secret fund, and, again, three names emerge: Mitchell, Stans, Magruder. That Magruder appears on both lists is a bit confusing, as is the fact that the amount of money in question keeps changing: the Government Accountability Office (GAO) report that Bernstein refers to mentions $350,000; the Bookkeeper claims as much as $6 million; and Sloan says $1 million. These inconsistencies establish a restricted narrative access, one that keeps full understanding just out of our reach.

On this matter, too, Woodward and Bernstein appealed to Redford: 'To eliminate confusion between Jane Alexander's references to 15 names on the list and five names, it would help if both references were to five – those who controlled the money' (Bernstein and Woodward 1975). In fact, even in the later draft of the script, this focus was clear. There, the first scene with the Bookkeeper made no mention of L, P and M. The focus was on the five men who were in control of the secret slush fund. The scene with Woodward and Bernstein at Woodward's apartment introduced L, P and M, but the focus was also primarily on the five men in control (something the film completely drops from that scene). So, in the script, the move to Sloan's house and a discussion of the five men in control of the fund flowed naturally from the previous scenes. In the film, it does not. The reporters' focus has suddenly shifted, a development that has occurred in between the scenes we see, but no explanatory reference is made to it.

The lack of clarity in this sequence produces in us not just some degree of confusion, but more importantly an awareness that we are getting only fragments of the overall story. Of course, classical cinema – which is marked by a continuity, cause and effect, 'utmost denotative clarity from moment to moment' (Bordwell 1985: 161) – also offers us a necessarily partial view of events. But the continuity system makes that partial view seem complete, in part because no relevant story issues are withheld from us. In this film, relevant story information that would create a clearer continuity is regularly withheld from us, and what we have instead is (by continuity standards) confusing and even contradictory. This sequence exemplifies the ways in which, throughout, the film's narration is marked by gaps, fissures, inconsistencies.

In dismissing Woodward and Bernstein's request for a more legible rendering of their investigation, Redford and Pakula intuited that a certain measure of obscurity wouldn't diminish the movie's urgency, but only enhance it. It was a crucial insight. In 1913, Bertrand Russell once objected that 'Wittgenstein often condensed his remarks to the point of impenetrability and failed to spell out the arguments in support of his claims. Doing so', Wittgenstein replied, 'would "spoil their beauty"' (Glock 2004: 434). Wittgenstein, in other words, saw philosophy as an *aesthetic* activity. Despite their own material's historical basis, Redford and Pakula agreed; they would also aestheticise, rearranging facts to improve their film. They made Woodward the first reporter to cover the break-in (it was actually *Post* police reporter Al Lewis, mentioned only in passing by Metro Editor Harry Rosenfeld [Jack Warden]) and Bernstein the first to contact Donald Segretti (it was a *Post* freelancer) (Downie 2020: 67–8, 77). To concentrate on Rosenfeld and Managing Editor Howard Simons (Martin Balsam), they eliminated Barry Sussman, who, as the *Post*'s District Editor, had actually directed the Woodward and Bernstein team. Deep Throat's dramatic warning of the danger to their lives occurred on 16 May 1973, the night before the Senate Watergate Committee began its hearings, not on the eve of Nixon's 20 January inauguration, where the film places it. And *ATPM*'s single most famous line, Deep Throat's advice to 'Follow the money', was an invention of scriptwriter William Goldman.

## Aestheticising: a dark street and brownstone houses, an opera house at 2.00 am

By playing fast and loose with spatial continuity, Pakula often suspends literal realism for aesthetic effects. Compare two scenes. The first (35:15) shows Woodward following Deep Throat's instructions for requesting a meeting: he places a red flag in a flowerpot on his apartment's balcony, framed by the convergence of three starkly modern, featureless buildings. Near its conclusion (2:05:24), the movie returns to this apartment, as Woodward is woken up by a phone call

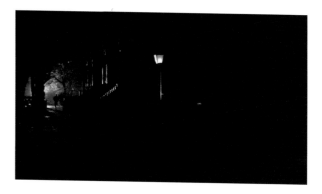

from Bernstein asking about Deep Throat. Woodward hangs up and
rushes to put on a jacket. The next shot shows him exiting a building's
front door and running alone, away from the camera, down a dark,
leafy, mysteriously deserted street, lined with brownstones.

This evocative, unrecognisable neighbourhood, with its wet
pavement and old-fashioned street lamps, seems entirely inconsistent
with the earlier scene's contemporary architecture *brut*. But it exactly
matches the sequence that follows, the ominous night cab ride to the
final Deep Throat rendezvous, set amid the multistorey car park's
ominous shadows. Pakula, in other words, has replaced spatial
continuity with *atmospheric continuity*.

The similar treatment of Woodward's first meeting with Deep
Throat suggests a deliberate film-making strategy. With a message
inserted into his home-delivered *New York Times*, Deep Throat
summons the reporter to a secret conference: 'Take precautions against
being followed,' the note reads. 'We will meet at 2.' The sequence
that follows shows Woodward riding in a cab to the Kennedy Center,
where he gets out to lose himself in a crowd leaving what the building's
sign identifies as 'Opera House'. But unless the opera happened to be
Wagner's *Die Meistersinger*, surely no performance would end this
late. (And what about the lone voice that emerges from the swarm of
people, unidentified, but clearly calling out, 'Good luck, Mr President'?
Is this well-heeled audience exiting a fund-raiser?) Pakula spent a

fortune on this shot (the movie's most expensive), hiring 1,500 extras and wetting the streets for a noir look (Boorstin 2016). For all the film's meticulous recreation of reality, in other words, the person making it proved repeatedly willing to abandon both continuity and credibility for the sake of an aesthetically powerful moment.

## Set design and clues: Woodward's crutch, Bernstein's banjo and the mystery of Pete Teller

George Jenkins and George Gaines built *ATPM*'s famous reproduction of the *Washington Post*'s enormous newsroom, creating a display case preserving the way of life of the 1970s *Washington Post*. Although some discussion took place about shooting at *The Post* itself, that arrangement would never have been possible. Instead, the designers built a slightly smaller newsroom on a Burbank soundstage, one with 160 desks instead of the actual 180 (Boorstin 2016). *Post* editor Leonard Downie, Jr recalls the preparation that went into that effort:

Pakula's production manager and his assistants … [took] 1,000 photographs. … They obtained the construction blueprints and measured everything. … they reproduced the main newsroom … with the same bright fluorescent overhead lighting, brightly colored furnishings, and glassed-walled offices along its perimeter.

Copies of the same works of art hung in the soundstage newsroom, along with 1972 calendars displaying the correct date for each scene. … The phones had the correct extension numbers on them, and 1972 phone directories were on the desks. All the equipment and technology worked. (Downie 2020: 102)

*The Post* supplied trash to fill the set's wastebaskets and scatter across its desks, and 'the actors playing reporters and editors in the background would be doing the appropriate things in every scene', their behaviour captured by Gordon Willis's extensive use of wide-angle lenses and deep-focus photography. Watching the movie, Downie recalled that 'At the beginning of each scene, I could tell the hour of the day and the day of the week by what was happening in the background' (Downie 2020: 102). *Post* editor Ben Bradlee visited the Burbank set and found himself flabbergasted by the exact likeness he encountered.

What effect results from this obsessive accumulation of details? Pakula clearly wanted *ATPM* to appear as realistic as possible, and although he never approved of Redford's original semi-documentary plan, the newsroom set owes something to that idea. In a documentary, however, the places filmed have an independent status; in a movie like *ATPM*, everything we see on screen *has been put there by the film-makers*. In general, commercial film-making prefers to work more economically. When historian Natalie Davis kept suggesting more and more 'Medieval' details for the movie version of her book *The Return of Martin Guerre* (1983), the film-makers invoked 'the camel principle': if you want a scene to register as 'Egyptian', they told her, you simply put a camel in one corner of the shot. Did *ATPM* need what its makers proudly called 'realistic trash'?

In *How Fiction Works* (2019), James Wood distinguishes between off-duty and on-duty details, with only the latter necessary to the story. Roland Barthes, on the other hand, saw a role for off-duty details, citing the barometer in Flaubert's 'A Simple Heart' (1877): it is precisely their *insignificance* that produces 'the realistic effect'. The realism of these 'futile', 'useless' details, Barthes argued, derives from the assumption of reality's inscrutability. This insight especially applies to the cinema. If a fiction writer has to intentionally summon the details she records, a film-maker can be surprised by something previously unnoticed, even on a carefully prepared set. André Bazin celebrated the dust kicked up from a country road by Renoir's Boudu, and D. W. Griffith revered the wind in the trees behind Lumière's baby – off-duty details achieving 'the realistic effect'. Thus, *ATPM*'s newsroom set raises these questions:

1. Which of the newsroom's details could be changed without affecting the film?

2. Does increasing the number of off-duty details make a movie more realistic? What if a film-maker chooses those details for exactly that purpose?
3. What would a movie that eliminates off-duty details be like? A fairy tale? A cartoon? A novel?

As a genre, the detective story enacts a meta-commentary on Wood's distinction. Conan Doyle's 'Silver Blaze' (1892), for example, turns on Sherlock Holmes's ability to distinguish between the details that count (the curried mutton, the silent dog) and those that don't (the scarf, the racing tout's attempted bribe). The tale's appeal, of course, results from reversing the reader's original classification. As another famous detective story, *Trent's Last Case* (E. C. Bentley, 1913), begins: 'Between what matters and what seems to matter, how should the world we know judge wisely?'

For something advertised as a detective story, *ATPM* depends very little on this problem. Woodward and Bernstein don't go down blind alleys; they don't have to distinguish between real and false clues. They simply have to get people to talk. Thus, when the *Post* receptionist impatiently tells Bernstein that 'Pete Teller' has called, without leaving a return number, the movie doesn't make us anticipate a fresh development; it simply reminds us of Bernstein's carelessness – he doesn't read his messages. He doesn't ask whether anyone recognises the name, nor does he check the CREEP directory. The film marks important names by prompting action: Woodward and Bernstein follow up, enquire about or confirm information about them (Cieslikowski 2021).

What does *ATPM* ask us to make of other details – the single bicycle wheel beside Bernstein's desk, the crutch in a corner of Woodward's apartment, the banjo in Bernstein's? Are they character devices, clues to their habits (Bernstein was an avid cyclist who biked to work), their histories (had Woodward suffered an unmentioned injury?) or abandoned hobbies (the banjo)? How would the movie change if the wheel and the crutch and the banjo went missing?

## Set design and the practical

Film-makers refer to something on a set that actually works as
'a practical', and *ATPM*'s functioning telephones, fax and teletype
machines are all examples. But what about the furniture and pictures
bought from Woodward to make his movie apartment a replica of
where he had once lived? Or Bradlee's books that decorate Robards's
office? Or the Bookkeeper's former house, rented for the movie
from its new owner? Or Bernstein's watch that Hoffman wore, or
the wallet the actor carried, whose contents exactly duplicated the
reporter's? Over fifty years before *ATPM*, Hollywood had decided
that this kind of obsessive attention to detail was *im*practical, a
conclusion forever associated with one name: Erich von Stroheim.
A vestige of the cottage industry, von Stroheim was used to having
his own way with the movies he wrote, directed and starred in, and
he became notorious for incidents like refusing to continue a picture
until a thousand champagne glasses with quarter-inch gold rims were
replaced with ones whose rims were precisely half an inch (Marx
1975: 33). Von Stroheim's most often-reported extravagance involved
his purchase of expensive silk underwear, worn by his actors playing
aristocrats, but never seen in the film. Doesn't Hoffman's wallet
amount to the same thing?

What prompts this mimetic overdrive? How can it matter if
*ATPM*'s version of Woodward's apartment has exactly the same
furniture as the real thing if a viewer has never seen the real thing?
Does such maniacal fidelity simply relieve *ATPM*'s set designers from
having to *invent* Woodward's apartment as the *Maltese Falcon*'s team
had to do for Sam Spade's? Does the actual existence of Woodward's
apartment, located in Washington at 1718 P Street NW, as opposed
to Spade's fictional one, require this effort? Do the utterly realistic
(real?) sets and objects enable the actors to enter more readily into
their roles? But didn't Shakespeare's actors do without any sets at all?

Note an important difference between the studio-built newsroom
and the Bookkeeper's house. Over its history, the cinema has
repeatedly been refreshed when film-makers are stimulated by reality's

refractory nature. See, for example, the case of the Italian Neorealists. Otto Preminger once explained the benefits of shooting *Anatomy of a Murder* (1959) in the original case's exact locations, including the courtroom and the defence attorney's home: the difficulties presented by confined or public spaces required his inventiveness. And the unexpected can prove useful. Having gained admittance into the Bookkeeper's house, Bernstein struggles to close the front door behind him, and Hoffman, improvising in the midst of a heavily staged scene, turns to her, saying, 'Door sticks.' The Bookkeeper's stubborn, real front door has provided the movie with a vivid summary of all the scenes of Woodward and Bernstein being turned away from one door after another – until Bernstein pushes his way through this one.

## Spatial and temporal discontinuities

After its credits, *ATPM* begins with four scenes:

1. The Watergate break-in.
2. The responses in the *Post* newsroom of Metro Editor Harry Rosenfeld and Managing Editor Howard Simons. Bernstein is briefly present.
3. The editor's call that wakes Woodward in his apartment.
4. Woodward's attendance at the courthouse arraignment of the five burglars.

Where are these four places in relation to each other? How much time elapses between the first scene and the second? Between the third and the fourth? The movie doesn't tell us. Its not doing so was not inevitable.

Because a feature-length film is an assemblage of shots and scenes, taken at different times and places, often in an order different from how they will appear on screen, the cinema has to deal with discontinuities of space and time. In *Theory of Film Practice* (1981: 3–16), Noël Burch provides a typology of possible articulations between Shot A and Shot B:

## Spatial articulations

1. Spatial continuity: Shot A's space overlaps with Shot B's.
2. Proximate discontinuity: Shot A's space is near Shot B's.
3. Radical spatial discontinuity: the two shots are set in entirely different spaces.

## Temporal articulations

1. The two shots are continuous, with Shot B beginning where Shot A ends.
2. A measurable temporal ellipsis, or time abridgement, between the two shots.
3. An indefinite ellipsis between the two shots.
4. A measurable time reversal or flashback.
5. An indefinite time reversal.

*ATPM*'s first four scenes exhibit radical spatial discontinuity: four entirely different locations, whose exact distances from each other are never revealed. As the film enters new locations, it will continue to withhold their relative locations. *ATPM* will show us the following places:

- the Watergate building
- the *Post* newsroom and editors' offices

- Woodward's apartment
- the courthouse
- an outdoor restaurant table
- the Library of Congress
- several street scenes, two with Woodward and Bernstein in a car
- the Kennedy Center
- the multistorey car park where Woodward meets Deep Throat three times
- an outdoor bench
- the State Attorney's office in Miami, FL
- seven houses where CREEP employees refuse to talk
- a fast-food restaurant
- the CREEP Bookkeeper's house
- Hugh Sloan's house
- a street next to the White House
- Donald Segretti's house in California
- Bernstein's apartment
- the FBI building
- Bradlee's house

In Burch's terms, shots juxtaposing these spaces are radically discontinuous, but the movie keeps us in the dark about their exact locations. It refuses to show us, for example, that Woodward's apartment was only a few blocks from *The Post*, and that Deep Throat's car park was across the Potomac in Rosslyn, VA. Despite how vividly they appear, except for the public buildings, we would not be able to draw a map of them.

The first four scenes also show *ATPM*'s temporal discretion. Each of the three transitions involves an indefinite ellipsis. But how much time has passed between the break-in and the second scene at *The Post*? Even the next transition, to a shot of the phone waking Woodward, is confusing, seeming to occur in the middle of the night – after all, the burglary scene had concluded in near darkness. Only on rewatching can we spot a daylit window that appears briefly in

Shot 2. How long does it take Woodward to get from his apartment to the courthouse? The movie doesn't tell.

Most commercial film-making doesn't work this way, even though virtually every narrative movie requires spatial discontinuities and temporal abridgements. Compare another opening four-scene sequence that involves a protagonist being woken by a phone call. In its first few minutes, *The Maltese Falcon* (1941) shows us:

1. Sam Spade's office
2. the corner of Bush and Stockton (and Lew Archer's murder)
3. Spade's apartment (where he gets the phone call)
4. the murder scene again

*The Maltese Falcon* (1941)

Although we can't precisely locate #2 relative to either #1 or #3, or tell exactly how much time has elapsed between scenes, the movie does offer clues. Scene 1 ends with Archer agreeing to shadow Brigid 'after 8 o'clock' that night, while in Scene 3, a bedside table clock shows 2.05 in the morning, as Spade tells his caller that he can reach the murder scene in fifteen minutes. Thus, we can conclude that the discovery of Archer's body has taken roughly six hours, and that Spade's apartment is relatively close to Bush and Stockton. Later in the movie, when Spade has been summoned by what turns out to be a fake call, he asks the cab driver, 'You got plenty of gas? Do you know where Ancho Street or Avenue is in Burlingame?', we know that he's in for a drive, but not one beyond the immediate San Francisco area. *ATPM*, by contrast, resembles a dream, a compendium of distinctly rendered, realistic spaces whose relation to each other eludes us.

## The newsroom I: the order of operations and the case of the moving desks

Having spent $450,000 to replicate the *Post* newsroom, the film-makers made sure to use it. *ATPM* returns repeatedly to shots of Woodward and Bernstein at their desks and the editors in their glass-walled perimeter offices. What's remarkable, however, is the movie's refusal to provide these sequences with conventional spatial orientation. Presented with continually changing camera set-ups, scenes involving axis crossings and the near invisibility of overlapping details, even the most diligent viewer would find it enormously difficult to draw a map of this place. Where, for example, are the editors' offices in relation to Woodward's desk? To Woodward's left? To his right? Ahead of him? Why and how does *ATPM* make it so hard to tell?

A thumbnail diagram of the *Post* set [opposite] will assist us in articulating the newsroom's spatial relations without minimising their obscurity.

The textbook order of operations dictates that a scene begins with an establishing wide shot (which orients the viewer to a new

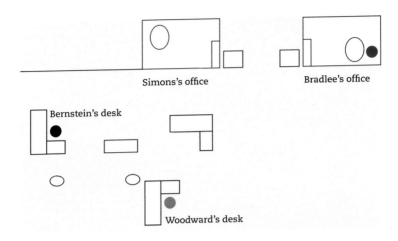

Simons's office                    Bradlee's office

Bernstein's desk

Woodward's desk

setting) before moving into medium shots and close-ups, and then
back out again – what Noël Burch dubbed the 'concertina style'. The
succession of these differently framed shots is rendered legible by
eyeline matches that respect the 180-degree axis of action presented in
the establishing shot. In addition, film-makers commonly find ways to
anchor scenes in the same location with distinctive set elements (e.g.
a lamp, a wall hanging) that remind us where we are in a previously
seen space. But director Pakula decided that such slavish devotion to
these filmic conventions would not suffice. Here in the *Post* offices,
such unusual filmic variation occurs that as soon as we *feel* familiar
with the newsroom space, new perspectives upset our orientation.

We first see the *Post* offices in a scene immediately following
the opening break-in sequence, as Simons walks across the main
newsroom and into Rosenfeld's office to share a story about a car
crash. The newsroom appears as a vast rectangular space filled with
rows of desks and filing cabinets, punctuated by a series of floor-to-
ceiling columns [next page].

Soon after, once Woodward learns the contents of the burglars'
address books, we cut to a close-up of him at his desk, speaking to
someone off screen: 'You can dial the White House direct, can't you?'

An unseen woman replies affirmatively, but her voice is mixed at a noticeably lower volume than Woodward's – an audio imbalance the film will repeatedly employ. Woodward then telephones the White House in an attempt to reach Howard Hunt. But we get no wider establishing shot that would allow us to situate him in relation to any part of the *Post* offices we've already seen, such as Rosenfeld's office, nor does the set-up include the colleague he questions. The close-up's shallow focus further removes Woodward from any surrounding context. These choices combine to create the feeling that we can't quite see as much as we want.

When Woodward's call concludes, he gets up from his desk to ask Rosenfeld about Colson, and this shot now serves as something

like the withheld establishing shot. This move respects the axis, as does his subsequent shot/reverse shot exchange with Rosenfeld. Woodward then returns to his desk for another series of phone calls, all of them presented with roughly the same close-up framing of him as before. Given that this second sequence of Woodward on the phone involves a series of temporal ellipses, we might expect variations in camera set-up or in Woodward's position at his desk, which would signal temporal gaps and provide renewed spatial orientation – but we get no such variations.

The scene in which Woodward discovers Bernstein rewriting his news stories depends on a masterful orchestration of continuity-based visual presentation that sees the camera move across the

established axis in a way that comfortably orients the viewer to the spatial relationship between the reporters' desks. The scene begins with a medium close-up of Woodward at his desk, a shot that respects the axis established in the earlier sequence [previous page]. He finishes typing, gets up and moves screen right, the camera panning with him as he walks a few feet away and drops the page in the Metro desk's basket. Bernstein is clearly visible at his desk in the background [above].

After returning to his desk, Woodward spots Bernstein picking up the pages he's just turned in. A series of reverse angles follow, with eyeline glances that make spatial orientation clear. Finally, after seeing Bernstein take another of the pages, Woodward gets up

from his desk, the camera tracking backward with him as he walks to Bernstein's desk, establishing a new 180-degree axis [above]. We then get a number of closer shot/reverse shots of the two reporters in a tense conversation, an 'adversarial' pattern that will yield to a reliance on two shots, which show them together in the same frame (Holmes 2018: 99).

The scene in which Bernstein telephones the White House Librarian respects the axis established in the previous scene of him at his typewriter arguing with Woodward; and when Bernstein gets up and moves to Woodward's desk [next page], the camera pans left and settles on a wide shot that, again, follows a previously established axis of orientation.

So far, so good. If, at this point, we feel we comfortably understand the spatial relationship between the reporters' desks within this larger newsroom space, that comfort will soon be upset. Indeed, the axis orientation established in these scenes is challenged soon after when Bradlee criticises their story on Howard Hunt and the White House Librarian. Following their visit to the Library of Congress, Woodward and Bernstein return to the *Post* newsroom to compose their story. We see the two reporters gathered with Rosenfeld around Bernstein's typewriter in a set-up that pushes at the left edge of the previously established axis of action. Next, we see a shot of Bradlee leaving his office and heading towards the trio, the camera tracking with him as he walks. When he arrives, the

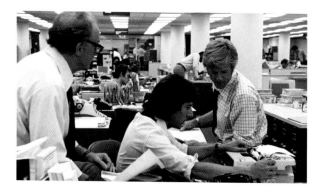

three others are in slightly different places, and the camera has moved to a new set-up, now on the opposite side of the established axis and off at an angle. The tracking shot of Bradlee carries us from the first shot of the reporters to the second, but the new set-up remains disorienting. Before, we knew exactly where Woodward's desk was in relation to Bernstein's. Where is it now in this second shot?

The establishment of new axes of action around previously established spaces continues. When Woodward telephones Kenneth Dahlberg, for example, we find ourselves in yet another new position in relation to him at his desk, now with the typewriter off to his left rather than in front of him.

In a later scene in which Bernstein telephones John Mitchell, we begin with a wide establishing shot that again adopts an unfamiliar angle on his desk, but the brevity of the shot does not give us sufficient time to orient ourselves. The following shot then offers a view of Bernstein that is so close, and taken in such shallow focus, that we cannot identify any surrounding set elements (if, indeed, there are any) that would suggest his exact location in the newsroom.

The variations continue. The scene with Sally Aiken (Penny Fuller) takes up still another new position at Woodward's desk. Indeed, we can't recognise that it is his desk until we see Woodward's nameplate over her shoulder.

In an essay on Carl Dreyer, Noël Burch considered that the common description of *La Passion de Jeanne D'Arc/The Passion of Joan of Arc* (1928) as a film consisting exclusively of close-ups, though clearly incorrect, somehow *feels* right. Burch explained that because Dreyer refuses to regularly orient the viewer with wide establishing shots that would provide a sense of where things are, and because he returns to the same spaces from unfamiliar perspectives, the viewer never arrives at a clear sense of the action's larger space: she never sees quite enough to know where the characters are. The barren walls of the prison cell and courtroom offer no orienting details (Burch 1980: 297–8). A variation on this practice appears in *ATPM*: unfamiliar perspectives on the reporters in the newsroom space, unsupported by any clear and consistent visual cues, make the characters appear as if floating, unmoored. Further, almost any perspective on the newsroom provides little orientation, only row after row of desks and typewriters, filing cabinets and columns – a setting not empty of details, but filled with too many, none of them distinctive enough to ground us. The helter-skelter editing and camera repositioning not only keep the viewer from getting comfortable; they also serve a mimetic function: they simulate a newsroom environment so hectic that Gordon Willis asked the reporters, 'How the hell do you work in this place?'

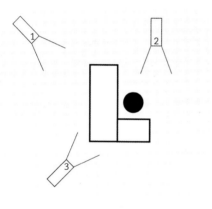

These diagrams indicate something of the range of perspectives from which we see the spaces of the two reporters' desks

**Bernstein's desk**
1. *Bernstein calls John Mitchell*
2. *Bradlee approves Mitchell story*
3. *Woodward and Bernstein argue*

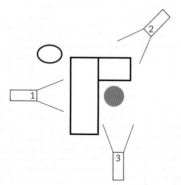

**Woodward's desk**
1. *Woodward calls Dahlberg*
2. *Woodward calls Hunt*
3. *Woodward and Bernstein talk to Sally Aiken*

## The newsroom II: in the background

Although the buzz of activity throughout the newsroom appears to be more or less random, unreadable, a distraction that contributes to the feeling of disorientation, this action, in fact, results from careful coordination on multiple levels. When former *Post* editor Leonard Downie, Jr saw the film, he was astonished by its accuracy: the choreography of the newsroom action was remarkably faithful to the paper's daily operations (Downie 2020: 102). This exactness resulted from design: Redford recalls that he and Pakula 'were constantly focusing on the [newsroom's] background', asking, 'what are *these* guys doing, what is their story? Some guy, way, way in the background. *Everybody* had to have a story' (Brown 2005: 182). In the film-makers' hands, the *Post* newsroom resembles a Bruegel painting that shows scores of figures engaged in a wide variety of activities.

Even for those without Downie's first-hand knowledge of the *Post* offices, attention to background action reveals the film's meticulous coordination of apparently marginal figures. As the reporters head out to the Library of Congress, Bernstein walks to his desk to get his jacket, and in the background left we can see Kay Eddy (Lindsay Crouse). At this point, she is not a specific character, just one of the many background figures in the newsroom. It is not until twenty minutes later that Woodward and Bernstein will approach her for help obtaining a list of CREEP employees.

In the following scene, after she drops the list on Woodward's desk, there is a shot/reverse shot of the two that confirms the position of Eddy's desk in relation to his. And in the background of Woodward's shot, we can see Sally Aiken, who will not emerge as a character in this drama for nearly an hour.

A similar complex coordination of foreground and background action – a balance probably noticed by few viewers – appears in the *fête* sequence of Jean Renoir's *La Règle du jeu/The Rules of the Game* (1939). As the action spins out of control on multiple fronts, the camera shows Robert and André carrying off the hysterical Geneviève, only to then pick up the gamekeeper Schumacher, who is in hot pursuit of Marceau, the poacher-turned-servant he believes

*La Règle du jeu* (1939)

has cuckolded him. As Schumacher races from one room to the next, wildly firing shots, we can, in the far background, glimpse Robert and André still in motion, now carrying Geneviève up the stairs. What appeared as chaotic activity now reveals itself as a carefully choreographed action designed to simulate randomness.

In *ATPM*, the random background action shows its design as background figures like Kay Eddy and Sally Aiken move to the foreground, rising from marginal to more important characters. Moreover, though much of what we see of the background activity remains simply incidental, its occasional promotion to the story's foreground makes us gradually become aware that *any* background action possesses this potential for a sudden change in significance. We sense that there is always action at the edge of our view capable of becoming relevant, but we can't know what or how. As with the investigation itself, information may suddenly emerge from anyone or from anywhere.

As Jared Brown indicates, this film-making strategy 'meant that the actors playing the editors ... needed to be on the set constantly, since they were frequently visible in the background (Brown 2005: 192). Perhaps the subtlest background appearance of a character in *ATPM* involves Ben Bradlee. The *Post* editor makes his big entrance thirty-one minutes into the film, but he is seen twice before. Viewers who recognise Jason Robards will spot him in long shot ten minutes

earlier, as he steps into Simons's office for a conference with his junior editors. But Bradlee is first seen five minutes before that, when he can be glimpsed in the extreme background of the scene in which Woodward asks Rosenfeld about Charles Colson. Through the interior full-length window of his office, Bradlee appears in a characteristic action, kicking his feet up on his desk and throwing his hands behind his head.

## The newsroom III: the editors' offices

The shot of Bradlee in the background should make clear to the viewer where his office is in relation to Woodward's desk (and thus also to Bernstein's). But variations of framing, character blocking, camera movement and lens use distort what should be a fairly clear arrangement of spaces. It takes careful examination to sort out the matter. And yet even when we do, we can still *feel* unsure.

Early in the film, two short scenes occur in Rosenfeld's office, but nothing clarifies its position relative to the reporters' desks. After these two scenes, we never again return to this location. Soon after, Woodward presents his reporting on Howard Hunt to Simons in his office, where Rosenfeld is also present. In the far background, we can see into what must be Bradlee's office: the framed illustration just off Woodward's left shoulder was there in Bradlee's first appearance, when Woodward and Rosenfeld discuss Colson.

Soon after the consultation with Simons, Woodward is back
at his typewriter. He glances up and at first appears to be in thought;
but then his eyes seem to settle, and we cut to a long shot of Simons,
National Editor Moffatt, Rosenfeld and Bradlee in Simons's office.
We can understand this long shot to be from Woodward's point of
view. In the previous scene, after Woodward left Simons's office,
Rosenfeld and Simons argued about whether the story would
remain with Woodward and Bernstein or be transferred to the
National desk. At the scene's conclusion, we hear Simons on his
phone saying, 'And see if Mr Bradlee is free. I want Ben to hear
this.' But when Woodward sees the men gathered in Simons's office,
he doesn't know they are having a discussion involving him, so he

registers no particular response. And his unfocused glance weakens
what should be a clear link between the two shots (and thus the
two spaces) and causes the wide shot of the men in the office to
register as oddly unanchored. Furthermore, our never returning to
Simons's office makes a precise assignment of its location all the
more difficult.

Still later, as we see Woodward and Bernstein with Rosenfeld,
working on their story about Howard Hunt and the White House
Librarian, we cut to a long shot of Bradlee in his office, picking
up his jacket. Again, the framed print on the top shelf appears
clearly. He passes through a small entryway and out into the
main newsroom. He moves out into the newsroom, pausing for

a low-angle close-up, and then moves on to the space of Bernstein's desk.

His path to the reporters here differs from another one taken later by Woodward and Bernstein, when they visit his office to confer about the CREEP slush fund. Further, if we compare the early shot when Woodward asks Rosenfeld about Colson (with Bradlee visible in the far background) with the shot when the reporters respond to Bradlee's angry summons, *the distance between the two spaces seems different*. And the yellow chairs that stand out so significantly in the foreground, which another director might have used as a visual anchor between the two locations, remain features of the set we've never been cued to notice.

The viewer's confusion about the spatial arrangement of the desks and offices in the *Post* newsroom is one aspect of the film's curious point-of-view system – if we use that term, as Douglas Pye presents it, to indicate the various ways in which a film both permits and restricts access to its story world. Of particular relevance here is Pye's assertion that 'the idea that limits imposed on the spectator's … access to the story are significant and highly variable is perhaps the central concept of point of view' (Pye 2000: 13). *ATPM* circumscribes such access not only by keeping some actions and events off screen, but also by variously limiting our knowledge of what we *do* get to see – concerning both plot events and physical space.

With the exception of the opening sequence of the break-in and a few brief scenes with *Post* editors, *ATPM* seems to offer a fairly conventional form of subjectively restricted narration, one marked by an epistemological alignment with Woodward and Bernstein. In other words, the film's narrational point of view is largely restricted to the reporters and their limited position of knowledge. This approach is typical of detective films, which routinely confine their narration to precisely this kind of epistemological subjectivity – with breaks in this alignment designed to give the viewer just enough extra information to generate some suspense (e.g. the scenes in which the editors discuss possibly removing Woodward and Bernstein from the story). But this film's point-of-view system is more complicated. As Douglas Pye has explained, the point of view of a given film (or even a single scene) consists of several 'axes': a temporal axis, which selects and orders story elements for presentation; a spatial axis, which organises the perspectives from which those selected events are presented to us, on a shot-by-shot basis; and a cognitive axis, which regulates the knowledge that characters have in relation to one another and also, importantly, the knowledge that the audience has in relation to the characters (Pye 2000: 10).

We have seen some of the ways in which *All the President's Men* seems to function according to this narrational logic of epistemological alignment, but actually it does not. There is a disturbance along the cognitive axis, caused first of all by gaps in the temporal axis – that is, by the ways the film withholds or elides plot information (making us feel at times that we know far less than the reporters). But there is also a disturbance along the spatial axis – not in one given scene, but in the collection of scenes set in the newsroom – that causes further cognitive disorientation.

One more example: When Woodward and Bernstein meet with their three editors to discuss whether they have sufficient proof of Haldeman's involvement, Bradlee paces slowly among the arguing newsmen in a space that registers as *somewhere* in the *Post* newsroom. When the scene concludes, and we cut back to the main newsroom as the reporters are exiting Bradlee's office, we realise that

the conversation has taken place in a previously unshown part of his office. Throughout the men's discussion, Pakula provided no visual cues (such as the framed print on Bradlee's bookshelf) that would have clarified where we were.

Cumulatively, these choices produce what, in a discussion of Ozu, Noël Burch described as 'a "jolt" in the editing flow, a moment of confusion in the spectator's sense of orientation to diegetic space, requiring a moment's readjustment' (Burch 1979: 159). In other words, *even in their movie's most important location*, ATPM's film-makers choose to keep viewers off balance, unsettled, confused – exactly the feelings Woodward and Bernstein had experienced. It's the Hemingway method in practice – and in a commercial movie. As one of our students remarked, 'I liked *ATPM*, but it was taxing. I really had to concentrate while I was watching it.'

## Interview framing

If the newsroom scenes rely more on regularly changing perspectives than on returning to established ones, their paired opposite is the interview sequences. These choices are remarkable. In both cases, the film-makers are rejecting precisely the standard ways of working. The newsroom's Bruegelesque complexity would seem to call for rigorous continuity, based on repeating set-ups made familiar to the audience. The interviews' duets and trios, on the other hand, would typically prompt shot variation, designed both to relieve the potential tedium of talking heads and to emphasise revelatory moments. Again, Pakula opts for something different.

In the scene where Bernstein interviews the Bookkeeper, the camera settles into a shot/reverse shot framing of the two that never varies, even as a lengthy conversation unfolds [next page]. Steven Soderbergh has remarked, 'Throughout the whole scene, the camera remains the same distance away from both of them. It never goes in for a close-up. It never changes the distance at all. By maintaining the same distance, it keeps the intensity building in the scene. Normally, you'd go in and out' (Brown 2005: 190).

Typically, camera movements in or out would not only offer visual variety, but would also, more importantly, highlight for the viewer moments of decisive narrative information or dramatic significance. Pakula refuses such signalling here, thereby making both the information and its significance harder for the viewer to assess. This approach also suggests the stubbornness of both the determined reporter and his reluctant source. But there is also another dynamic in play: Woodward and Bernstein's investigations depended on extracting information from people who were too afraid, or too loyal, or too ashamed to talk. Thus, their interviews resembled confessionals (Boorstin 1995: 160) or Freudian sessions, in which any overt response to a subject's inadvertent bombshell might abruptly halt the flow of information. In the movie, the reporters' poker-faced attention is replicated by Pakula's deadpan editing. Neither the journalists' sources nor the film's viewers will get tripped into high alert.

The Bookkeeper sequence is not unique. In virtually all the scenes where the reporters question a potential source, Pakula takes the same approach, beginning with the first sequence of Woodward at his desk, telephoning the White House in an attempt to reach Howard Hunt. We see Woodward in a medium close-up, picking up the phone and dialling. This first section consists of five shots, alternating between the medium close-up of Woodward and a close-up of his notepad as he scribbles notes, in a temporally continuous sequence.

After this call, Woodward walks over to Rosenfeld to ask about
Charles Colson, before returning to his desk to make more calls.
There follows a sequence of fifteen shots – again alternating between
the medium close-up of Woodward and close-ups of his notepad. This
sequence is temporally discontinuous: it consists of a series of calls
to several different potential sources. The framing, however, never
changes. This fixed-frame approach continues in Bernstein's meeting
with Sharon Lyons at the outdoor restaurant, and in all the scenes
with Deep Throat.

One notable variation occurs in what is perhaps the most
noticeable example of the fixed-frame approach, in the reporters'
first conversation with Hugh Sloan, in his living room. Woodward

and Bernstein appear in a wide shot, seated far apart, with Sloan
in a medium wide shot seated in a wingback chair [previous page].
But in contrast to the other scenes, this one ends with a cut to a
closer shot of Sloan – a cut-in that perhaps suggests he might not
be telling them the truth. In contrast to most readily legible
commercial cinema, however, this signal remains ambiguous – as
it must. Any decisive signalling here that Sloan is lying would itself
be a lie: he is not.

## Casting IV – the supporting parts

Many of the greatest movies benefit from indelible performances
by supporting actors. *Casablanca* (1942), for example, depends
not only on the Bogart–Bergman pairing, but also on S. Z. Sakall,
Peter Lorre, Dooley Wilson, Sydney Greenstreet, Claude Rains and
Conrad Veidt – character actors who work in a Dickensian mode.
They are types, in E. M. Forster's terms, 'constructed round a single
idea or quality', and thus instantly recognisable when they reappear
(Forster 1985: 67–8). As what Forster called 'flat characters', they
are memorable precisely because of their lack of complexity. They do
not surprise.

Some of *ATPM*'s roles are in this tradition. Martin Balsam's
sceptical Managing Editor Simons and Jack Warden's supportive
Metro Editor Rosenfeld seem as reliable as Mr Micawber's wife,
with her single mantra, 'I will never desert Mr Micawber.' (Warden
was between Oscar nominations for *Shampoo* [1975] and *Heaven
Can Wait* [1978]; Balsam had actually won ten years earlier for
*A Thousand Clowns* [1965].) Other characters seem even more
stock: Ned Beatty's slimy politician ('Caught me on my worst day')
and Polly Holliday as his smarmy secretary ('Mr Bern*stine*') are
caricatures, as is Nicolas Coster's Markham ('I'm not here'), the
evasive lawyer at the burglars' arraignment. On the other hand,
Penny Peyser (Sharon Lyons: 'My girlfriend told me to watch out for
you'), Penny Fuller (Sally Aiken: 'I guess I don't have the taste for the
jugular you guys have'), Stephen Collins (Hugh Sloan: 'My name's

been in the papers too much') and Robert Walden (Donald Segretti: 'I'm a good lawyer, and I'll probably end up going to jail and being disbarred') individualise their characters: we would be hard pressed to describe any of them in one or two words. With her sweat-stained armpits and nervous attempt to joke about John Mitchell's raincoat-over-his-head appearance at CREEP headquarters ('I thought he was going to go oohoo, oohoo'), Valerie Curtin makes reluctant witness Betty Milland more particular than any mere type. And in her first picture, Lindsay Crouse rounds Kay Eddy, who initially refuses Woodward and Bernstein's request that she 'use a guy I care about' to get the CREEP employee's list, before later tossing it on Woodward's desk without a word.

What about the three big character parts, Deep Throat (Hal Holbrook), Ben Bradlee (Jason Robards, Jr) and the Bookkeeper (Jane Alexander)? Deep Throat seems the flattest, emerging as reluctantly more forthcoming, but without ever abandoning a self-righteous cynicism and misanthropy ('I don't like newspapers. I don't care for inexactitude and shallowness') that may have motivated the real man, Mark Felt, who had been disappointed at being passed over for the FBI's top position. Presented with such a small part, Holbrook initially refused it, until Redford correctly convinced him of its importance. With his cracker-barrel Midwestern drawl, Holbrook proved an ideal fit for Missouri's Mark Twain, whom he portrayed on and off in a one-man show for sixty years. But though he also played US presidents, Holbrook often appeared as a villain, and his homespun accent and craggy features could easily turn sinister. Almost certainly, the solo Twain show had sharpened the timing he uses so effectively as Deep Throat, where he alternates crucial lines with stony silences in the face of Woodward's questions. Holbrook also had a habit of appearing to run out of wind at the end of a long speech, as if he couldn't allow himself to breathe until the torrent of words had finished. Listen to his unsupported breathlessness in this sequence's last sentence:

They bugged, they followed people, false press leaks, fake letters. They
canceled Democratic campaign rallies. They investigated Democratic private
lives. They planted spies, stole documents, and so on. Now, don't tell me you
think this is all the work of little Don Segretti.

For playing Ben Bradlee, Jason Robards won the Oscar for
Best Supporting Actor, a triumph he would repeat the next year as
Dashiell Hammett in *Julia* (1977). Robards had come to prominence
in the theatre, specialising in plays by Eugene O'Neill: *Long Day's
Journey into Night*, *Hughie*, *A Moon for the Misbegotten*, *A Touch
of the Poet*, *The Iceman Cometh* and *Ah, Wilderness!* But he had
fallen on hard times after a serious car wreck (probably caused by
his increasingly debilitating alcoholism) left his face scarred and his
reputation damaged. Redford, however, recalled Robards's generosity
from the days, early in the younger man's career, when both had
been in a television production of *The Iceman Cometh*. Robards
desperately wanted the Bradlee part, telling Pakula, 'I look like Ben
Bradlee, I sound like Ben Bradlee, and I've got to play Ben Bradlee'
(Brown 2005: 162). He signed for only $50,000, but the film revived
his career.

Robards had never quite become a movie star. His biggest part,
as disaffected, non-conformist, unemployed screenwriter Murray
Burns in *A Thousand Clowns* – a role he had initiated on Broadway –
had been a modest hit, but Robards himself kept getting shut
out of the big prizes. (The theatre version won a Tony for Sandy
Dennis, and the movie an Oscar for Martin Balsam.) Having him
play Ben Bradlee, however, amounted to one of those miracles of
casting – like W. C. Fields's Mr Micawber or Humphrey Bogart's
Rick Blaine – where actor and character perfectly coincide. Stanley
Cavell (1979) identified this alignment as peculiarly cinematic: if a
theatrical role resembles a position in a game, infinitely renewable
(a lot of different people can play third base, or Hamlet), a movie
character lives and dies with the star who created it. This proposition
would account for Tom Hanks's disastrously hammy attempt at

Bradlee in *The Post* (2017). But Micawber and Rick are fictional characters; Bradlee was a real person, alive and appearing regularly on talk shows. Most star performances amount to personification: the star embodies the character, often by budging not at all from his or her established persona. (Think of John Wayne, Clint Eastwood or Katharine Hepburn.) The apparent effortlessness of Robards's Bradlee, especially compared to Hanks's version, seems at first glance an example of personification: Robards just happened to *be* what most people thought Ben Bradlee was like. He was the right age (just one year younger), similarly craggy and profane, equally at ease in a dinner jacket or in shirtsleeves with his feet on a desk. But Robards was an actor, after all, and some of his performance involved impersonation. *Post* reporter Sally Quinn, who later married Bradlee, noticed this aspect:

I was just blown away by how accurate [Jason Robards] was, how he really got Ben. ... There was one moment when Ben comes into the newsroom, and he's in black tie and they've got this story they want to run. Ben reads it and throws it back on the desk and says, 'Run that baby.' And as he's walking out of the newsroom, he smacks his hands [and slaps a desk], you know like 'yes!' It was such a Ben gesture, and Jason just – I don't know where he got it, whether he saw Ben do it or whether he made it up or not. But it was just perfect. (Gaynor 2016)

Bradlee himself noticed the same moment: 'I wasn't conscious of making that gesture, but people say I did it a lot, and Alan had obviously seen me do it' (Brown 2005: 192).

Robards appears for barely sixteen of *ATPM*'s 138 minutes, and yet you can't forget him. Does he make Bradlee a flat or a round character? Redford describes Bradlee as 'a tough, edgy kind of guy': 'There's something of the star about Ben – legitimately. He's very, very charismatic, has a very powerful personality, is a real leader, and is thoroughly admired by everybody, including me' (Brown 2005: 161). In the movie, however, Bradlee doesn't change, with even his eventual willingness to print the Woodward–Bernstein stories resulting not from a shift in his own attitude but from their final conformity to his standards. The Bradlee of *ATPM* is a Dickensian character – flat, comic, vivid. And, miraculously, Bradlee may have been like that in real life, as Redford describes him: 'I don't know that he runs too deep because he's in a business that doesn't run too deep. It runs fast and doesn't have the time to go deep. But I have enormous respect for his guts and his ability. And he is great fun to be with' (Hirshberg 1976: 115).

Jane Alexander arrived for her first scene as the unnamed Bookkeeper (Judy Hoback Miller) without make-up, in an ordinary summer dress. She expected a costume change, but Pakula said she looked fine and hurried her into the shoot. Her performance over the next seven minutes confirms that film acting is an analogue activity, its emotional register shifting gradually, continuously, almost undetectably from one second to another, as her character hovers between a need to confess and a resistance to doing so. Her response to Bernstein's probing presence is elusive, evading any attempt to fix it with a single word. She first appears in an adjacent room, seen through the bannister railings, like a shy deer in the forest, but one who is also stubborn and sullen. In response to Bernstein's question, her reply ('I never worked for Sloan or Stans') comes as a smug so-there. She is wary, resistant, suspicious, exasperatedly raising her eyebrows towards her sister, who offers a cup of coffee to the reporter

she wants rid of. 'Sure you can sit down, but I'm not going to tell you anything.' She comes forward, averting her gaze to avoid looking at Bernstein, then sitting down on a sofa's front edge, hands in her lap, like a prim schoolgirl waiting to be asked to dance. 'I'm just curious why you lied just then,' Bernstein asks. 'Have you been threatened if you tell the truth?' She answers, 'No.' A pause, then, 'Never in so many words.' When the reporter tries to soften her up by asking about Mrs Stans's hospitalisation, he gets no reply. After a pause, she announces, 'I, I don't want to say any more, OK?', as she leans back against the sofa.

Throughout the scene, Alexander's stillness contrasts with Hoffman's busy fussing with his cigarette, coffee and notepad. Thus, any of her movements, however slight, become dramatic indications of the Bookkeeper's fluctuating attitude. When asked about the funds CREEP received, Alexander delivers the line 'There was so much of it' with an ironic smirk. 'I thought it was all legal,' she continues, leaning forward again. 'It's all so rotten,' she goes on, with a tiny head shake. 'It's getting worse,' now looking down and shaking her head again like an exhausted hall monitor. 'And the only one I care about is Hugh Sloan.' When Bernstein asks whether Sloan is being set up as a fall guy for John Mitchell, she looks down, her eyes covered with her left hand: 'If you guys could get John Mitchell, that would be beautiful.' As she looks up, she brings her right fist up to her chin, but allows any defiance to melt into timidity and apprehension about what she has revealed. Asked about records being destroyed, she becomes ironic: 'I think Gordon did a lot of shredding.' Her initial wariness returns as Bernstein probes about the men who controlled the secret fund. 'I don't want to say any more, OK?' she answers with a final, concluding gesture: she leans back against the sofa, with her arms and hands at her side.

Pakula recalled that shooting Alexander's two scenes, especially the first, was 'one of the most exciting weeks I've ever had filming anything' (Brown 2005: 190). Alexander had a similar response: 'The first scene with Dustin is my absolute favorite that I have ever filmed' (Gaynor 2016). In just seven minutes, she had accomplished an extraordinary feat: she had taken an absolutely stock character, the spinster bookkeeper (cousin to the maiden librarian), and made her come to life. Alexander received an Academy nomination for Best Supporting Actress, losing to Beatrice Straight, a performance now little remembered.

## The blank screen

The film's qualities of illegibility appear at the beginning. Or is it before the beginning? We can't be sure which it is. After the opening Warner Bros. logo has appeared, we expect the film to start. Instead, there follows an eighteen-second shot of a blank grey-white screen. We keep expecting the film to begin, but it keeps on not beginning. In a darkened theatre, this eighteen seconds of nothingness feels much longer. At some point, viewers commonly start to ask themselves: What's going on? Is this part of the movie? Is something wrong? Is the projector broken? This opening shot – *Is it a shot?* – situates the viewer in precisely the position of uncertainty and perplexity that its protagonists will occupy throughout the film. It is the first step in simulating their experience for the viewer.

Then suddenly: *Crack!* We get an extreme close-up of a typewriter key hitting paper. 'June 1, 1972', the explosion created by mixing the sounds of a cannon, a bullwhip and six typewriters

(Boorstin 2016). Each letter hits with the same force as the first. Only now are we certain that the film has begun.

## The man in the hotel room

The narrative and visual strategies of the scenes where Woodward and Bernstein begin their investigations, and the way those strategies position the spectator in a clouded cognitive relationship to story information, are anticipated by the film's opening break-in sequence.

In stark contrast to the white screen that opened the film's prologue, the story proper begins on a nearly black screen, also silent except for the quiet scratching of the burglars picking a Watergate lock. The night watchman discovers the taped door and alerts the police. As the burglars enter the Democratic National Committee headquarters, one pulls a walkie-talkie from his jacket pocket and announces, 'Unit One to Unit Two. We're home.' A high-angle long shot then shows the undercover police pulling to a stop in front of the Watergate building and jumping out of their car.

Until this point, the sequence has developed as a well-handled version of a cops-and-robbers tale. But then, at roughly the midpoint of this 4'45" scene, we are shown a man in a hotel room. His appearance, in the twelfth of the sequence's thirty-one shots, is motivated by the previous shot of the police arriving, which we

now understand – retroactively – to be from his point of view, an
awareness confirmed by the slightly low-angle long shot of him
in the hotel room, taking a step forward in response to their arrival.
He speaks into a walkie-talkie: 'Base One to Unit One. We have some
activity here. Silence is advised.' Hearing this warning, the burglars
shut off their own device.

For much of the rest of the sequence, the man in the hotel
room tries in vain to alert the burglars to the dangers that he sees but
they cannot. This man, the person in the sequence who speaks the
most, is, like us, an observer, watching the events unfold across the
street. Like him, we know more than the burglars and more
than the police – but we know less *about him* than we know about
those others. They are types (police and criminals), but the man in
the hotel room remains unidentified; indeed, he seems little more
than a figure with a voice. The camera gets close physically to the
other characters in the sequence, but never to him. He is always held
at a distance.

The man makes only three more appearances in the sequence,
each anchored by a shot marked as his point of view of the Watergate
building from the hotel room across the street. His voice is audible
only when he is on screen or during a shot recognisable as coming
from his point of view. But when the view of the building's exterior first
appeared (in the sequence's second shot), nothing signalled that it was a

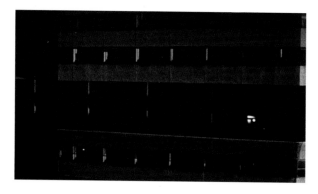

character's point of view. The man who is its anchor would not emerge for two full minutes – but he was there, prompting it.

The view cinema presents us with is always partial, but the partial vision we have here is a particular kind described by Pascal Bonitzer:

Technically speaking, filmic space is divided between two fields: on-screen space and off-screen space; we could say, between specular space and blind space. Specular space is on-screen space; it is everything we see on the screen. Off-screen space, blind space, is everything that moves (or wriggles) outside or under the surface of things, like the shark in *Jaws*. If such films 'work,' it is because we are more or less held in the sway of these two spaces. [...] In other words, if a film produces, as it is said to do, a strong impression of reality, it is less because of photographic realism and movement than because it presents a dialectic between these two spaces (or fields). (Bonitzer 1981: 58)

This dialectic accounts for why the man in the hotel room proves so unsettling: it is not just that the movie refuses to identify him; it's that he was there *before we knew he was there*. His belated appearance reminds us that as film spectators, our view is always incomplete, forcing us to reconsider what we previously saw and (thought we) understood.

The man in the hotel room is not the only unknown figure. When he calls the burglars on his walkie-talkie, he says, 'Base One to Unit One.' But when the burglars enter the DNC office, they call, 'Unit One to Unit Two.' *Who is Unit Two? And where is he?* He remains both unknown and unseen.

From here on, *ATPM* makes its off-screen space an active field, and as its brief on-screen representative, the man in the hotel room stands in for what comes to be the reporters' abiding fear: that they are being watched by shadowy, unknown figures, somewhere outside the frame of the story as they have it, who see more and know more than they – or we – do.

## The investigation begins

*Mise-en-scène* choices also shape the film's distinctive point-of-view system and contribute to its intermittent near illegibility. In his first official investigative act, Woodward visits the court to report on the arraignment of the Watergate burglars. The scene, consisting of a single shot and lasting a mere twenty-six seconds, demands an unusual amount of perceptual effort from the viewer.

Woodward enters the mysteriously dark courthouse lobby from the rear, and then takes up a position talking with a small group of lawyers. On the one hand, our eyes can track Woodward because he enters beneath a patch of white light that draws our eye, he wears a much lighter suit than the other men and, of course, he's

played by Robert Redford. Beyond these focusing factors, however, the shot contains a remarkable amount of 'noise'. Woodward and the other figures are kept in the middle distance, and most of them have their backs to the camera or are otherwise obstructed from our view. People repeatedly pass in the foreground, interrupting and distracting us from the pertinent exchange. As Woodward asks questions, it is difficult to hear the responding man's replies, since his voice is mixed at a lower volume than Woodward's. The shot makes it almost as difficult to determine which of the men is speaking. The visual presentation here results in a strikingly *uncentred* shot. Our eyes are free – indeed, encouraged by distractions – to wander in the cluttered, busy frame, but our perspective is uncomfortably restricted by the unvarying camera set-up. Pakula provides none of the typical shot/reverse shot pattern that would centre our gaze, clarify the information offered or align us more intimately with Woodward's character. Though it is obvious what we should be focusing on – Woodward's exchange with the other man – we can begin to feel that among the distractions, something important might be escaping our attention. The scene's visual presentation asks us to focus, but its distractions make doing so difficult.

This scene/shot thus stands as what we could call, after George Wilson (1986), a 'rhetorical figure of narrational instruction'. In such moments, the scene's visual organisation presents not just the script's dramatic action, but also the film's primary thematic concern – here, the complications of perception in a world whose previously clear moral landscape has turned disturbingly opaque. In this way, again, the scene simulates the reporters' own experience. What is most important is often partly concealed in an ambiguous world that the viewer, like the protagonists, must attend to with the greatest care.

This scene of Woodward at the courthouse has its paired scene soon after, when Bernstein is officially assigned to the story and meets with Sharon Lyons, the young woman who had worked with Hunt and Colson. In Woodward and Bernstein's book, this conversation takes place on the phone; the script moves it to somewhere outdoors. Pakula, however, chose to shoot the scene on a restaurant's outdoor patio overlooking the city, in the flight path of planes arriving at and departing from Washington's National Airport; Bernstein's conversation with the young woman is repeatedly interrupted by the deafening sounds of jet engines. Here again, both Bernstein's and the viewer's attempts to gather facts about White House and CREEP activities must contend with noise (literal here) that threatens to drown out the vital information.

One question lingers: Why would anyone open a restaurant in such a location? But given that we never see the jets, only hear them, might we assume that Pakula added the noise later and instructed the actors to imagine it? If we recall that the audio interruptions in *Close-Up*'s (1990) powerful final scene were, in fact, contrived by Abbas Kiarostami, we can't help wondering if here, too, the scene's element that registers as its most realistic may have been fabricated, and not simply recorded.

## Pairs I

The film's opening – from silence/blank screen to loudness/full screen – also initiates *ATPM*'s organising strategy, the deployment of *paired oppositions*, prompted from the start by Redford's fascination with the Woodward–Bernstein odd couple:

I read this ... article on who these two guys were. It said, well, one guy is a Jew, the other guy is a WASP. One guy's a Republican, the other one is a liberal. One guy writes very well, the other guy doesn't write so well. They don't like each other, but they have to work together. I thought, 'That's really an interesting dynamic.' (Gaynor 2016)

*ATPM* is full of pairs and matches, complements and oppositions, pairs that become oppositions, and these circulate among characters, scenes and actions. Any individual character or scene can often be paired or opposed with more than one other. Some examples:

## Paired/opposed characters

- Woodward and Bernstein
- two editors: Simons and Rosenfeld (one sceptical, one supportive)
- two key sources: the Bookkeeper and Sloan (two honest CREEP employees who became entangled in the cover-up)
- Sloan and Donald Segretti (one honest, one corrupt)
- the Bookkeeper (Bernstein's source) and Deep Throat (Woodward's source)
- the two female *Post* reporters with White House connections: Kay Eddy and Sally Aiken

## Paired scenes

- two interviews with Sloan
- two interviews with the Bookkeeper
- two Bernstein meetings with Joe, the FBI agent
- two shots of a mysterious car delivering multiple copies of *The Post* to the White House
- two editorial meetings
- two scenes of Woodward and Bernstein together in a car
- two overhead shots of Woodward's car leaving the *Post* parking lot
- one scene with Kay Eddy (who delivers the list of CREEP employees), one with Sally Aiken (who reveals that Ken Clawson boasted of writing the Canuck letter)
- Bradlee's rejection of the first story ('You haven't got it') vs. his approval of the Mitchell story ('Run that baby')
- two hypotheticals (Bernstein on inferring a cover-up: 'If there's music playing in the car for ten minutes, and there's no commercial, what can you deduce from that? Is it AM or FM?') (Woodward on inferring Haldeman's involvement: 'If you go to bed at night, and there's no snow on the ground, when you wake up, and there's snow on the ground, you can say it snowed during the night, although you didn't see it.')

In places, Pakula makes a pairing almost unnoticeable. Having condescendingly explained to Woodward that Charles Colson is Special Counsel to the President, Rosenfeld further characterises him:

> There's a cartoon on his wall. The caption reads, 'When you got 'em by the balls, their hearts and minds will follow.'

Woodward has pinned to *his* wall, next to his desk, a quotation attributed to Winston Churchill from 1901:

> It does not matter how many mistakes one makes in politics, so long as one keeps on making them. It's like throwing babies to the wolves: once you stop, the pack overtakes the sleigh. This explains why the present administration prospers.

## Pairs II – dialectics

The Woodward–Bernstein/Redford–Hoffman contrasts prompted the basic structure of what Noël Burch would call the film's *dialectics*: the controlled opposition of cinematic variables. The movie's beginning indicates the two most obvious: *Silence vs. Noise* and *Darkness vs. Light*. The movie will persistently oppose the brightly lit newsroom's comforting hubbub of clattering typewriters, shouting voices and ringing telephones to the menacing silence of deserted city streets at dawn and an ominously dark, empty multistorey car park. If Pakula lacked a stylistic signature, so important to auteur critics, cinematographer Gordon Willis did not. Having shot both *Godfather* movies and Pakula's *Klute*, he had acquired the nickname 'The Prince of Darkness'. For *ATPM*, however, Willis worked equally hard on reproducing the actual *Post* newsroom's harsh, even, fluorescent lighting, notorious for its intrusive hum and poor colour rendition. He used, as he remembered, '135 miles of wire to route the units [the ballasts that run the fluorescent tubes] away from the lamps and to the outside of the stage wall, where they were enclosed in air-cooled boxes. All in all, I think, there were seven hundred fluorescent units and some fourteen hundred ballasts' (Willis 1976). He assigned the colour correction to the lab.

As *ATPM* progresses, with the two reporters working by themselves on the Watergate story, the bright, bustling newsroom increasingly seems a safe haven from the city's dark silence. The chaotic mess of Woodward's and Bernstein's dimly lit bachelor apartments – which anticipates that of groundskeeper Carl Spackler (Bill Murray) in *Caddyshack* (1980), who tidies with a leafblower – renders them as solitaries like Edward Hopper's urban loners. Both are at home only in the newsroom, only when working. With the exception of the married Hugh Sloan, the reporters' sources are also *isolés*: Segretti and Betty Milland appear to live by themselves, and the Bookkeeper with just a sister. Away from work, they seem more vulnerable, more willing to talk. Woodward had sensed the opportunity:

Your inclination is to see somebody in their office. But you usually do twice as well if you can get to see them in their homes. ... No phone calls. No appointments. If you ever take one of those interviews and graph it to plot the useful information against the amount of time you spend in someone's home, you'll find the useful information comes at the end of a long interview. (Downie 2020: 74)

*ATPM*'s skilful pacing makes it easy to forget just how much of the movie involves the reporters interviewing people. In fact, they have twenty-six conversations with sources or potential sources. Nine of these take place on the telephone:

Telephone interviews – Woodward (W) or Bernstein (B)
1. Howard Hunt (W)
2. Mr Bennett (about Hunt) (W)
3. The White House Librarian (B)
4. Ken Clawson (W)
5. Kenneth Dahlberg (W)
6. Clark MacGregor (W)
7. John Mitchell (B)
8. Ken Clawson (again) (W)
9. 'guy in Justice' (B)

The other seventeen are conducted in person:

In-person interviews – Woodward/Bernstein (W/B), day/night, inside/outside, home/office/neutral space
1. Sharon Lyons (B, day, outside, neutral space)
2. Telephone company employee (B, day, outside, neutral space)
3. Martin Dardis (Florida State Attorney) (B, day, inside, office)
4. Betty Milland (W&B, night, outside, home)
5. Betty Milland (W&B, night, outside, home)
6. Mrs Hambling (W&B, night, outside, home)
7. Carolyn Abbott (false lead) (W&B, night, inside, home)
8. Bookkeeper (B, night, inside, home)
9. Bookkeeper (W&B, day, outside, home)
10. Hugh Sloan (W&B, day, inside, home)
11. Hugh Sloan (W&B, night, inside, home)
12. Joe (FBI) (B, day, outside, neutral space)
13. Joe (FBI) (W&B, day, inside, office corridor)
14. Donald Segretti (B, day, inside and outside, home)

15. Deep Throat I (W, night, inside, neutral space)
16. Deep Throat II (W, night, inside, neutral space)
17. Deep Throat III (W, night, inside, neutral space)

Woodward's key source, of course, was Deep Throat, another lone wolf, later identified as Mark Felt, the FBI's Deputy Director. In *ATPM*, Woodward meets Deep Throat three times, all at night in the car park, a setting that played to Gordon Willis's strengths. Famous for his extreme chiaroscuro effects, Willis also liked sparse decors. 'There's always too much shit on the set, too much stuff on the table,' he complained. 'What you should be doing is taking things out, not putting things in' (Mikulec). Presented with the starkly empty, shadowy multistorey car park, he must have licked his chops. In fact, with its grid layout, floor-to-ceiling pillars and fluorescent lights (however few), the car park looks like an abandoned *Post* newsroom – no desks, no typewriters, no people – just the way Willis liked it, dark and dead quiet. Nathan Holmes called it 'the dark office', 'the newsroom's haunting double' (Holmes 2018: 101).

Taken together, the three Deep Throat sequences show Pakula's skill in theme-and-variation, as he re-harmonises the refrain, Woodward's conversations with his crucial source. At 5'26", the first is the longest, primarily because of its overture, the reporter's cab ride

and Kennedy Center taxi change, the arrival at the car park (rendered like an abstract painting) and the thirty-six seconds he spends in the car park before discovering Deep Throat – accompanied by David Shire's eddying, mysterious score, which, like Brian Eno's ambient music, seems always arriving. Only in this first meeting do we see Deep Throat before Woodward does, in a nearly totally dark close-up, with light reflecting from his pupils. In a staging the movie will repeat in the next two Deep Throat scenes, he startles Woodward *from behind*, here with the sound of his cigarette lighter. The reporter turns around suddenly, looking off screen, until Pakula cuts to a full shot of Deep Throat, hidden by the darkness, with all but the lighter invisible – a shot that Willis must have known recalls the effect William Daniels achieved in *Flesh and the Devil* (1926).

When Woodward enters the frame, we get one of the only two times in the three sequences when both men appear in the same shot. (The other occurs in the second.) What follows are eighteen shots of back-and-forth cutting between them, with Pakula always returning to the same set-ups, as if he wanted to make a simple tune memorable by repetition. The conversation's editing, however, avoids the mechanical; the cuts don't rigidly align sound to image, instead allowing one speaker's voice to continue *after* the shot has changed to his listener. Thus, when Deep Throat offers his famous advice to 'Follow the money', his words come from off screen; the camera is on

Woodward listening. The sequence ends abruptly with a direct cut to a *New York Times* headline, 'Calls to G.O.P. Unit Linked to Raid on the Democrats'.

The second Deep Throat sequence initiates the variations. By opening with a direct cut from Donald Segretti to Woodward standing alone in the car park's darkness, the scene eliminates the overture. It will, however, make more use of the *Silence/Noise* and *Darkness/Light* contrasts. As in their first meeting, Deep Throat surprises Woodward from behind, announcing himself with a challenge: 'What's the topic for tonight?' Willis uses a new key light, allowing the source's right eye, cheekbone and forehead to emerge from the darkness (Knudsen 2021), perhaps to visualise his greater willingness to talk.

That cooperativeness will now require twenty-eight shots, all but one two shot occurring in eyeline-matched cross-cutting. Pakula emphasises some of Deep Throat's lines by having the camera on him as he speaks: 'Did you change cabs?' 'Don't you understand what you're on to?' 'You're missing the overall.' On the sequence's twenty-eighth shot, the sound of a car starting shatters the car park's silence like a gunshot. In paired shots, both Woodward and Deep Throat turn their heads sharply to look off screen, but in different directions. The suspicious car leaves, tyres squealing, and we see Woodward's face enveloped in darkness except for his eyes. When he turns to look back, Deep Throat has vanished.

At this point, Pakula introduces a new variation, a nine-shot, nearly two-minute coda that reprises the scene's structuring oppositions. Four initial shots show Woodward leaving the car park, the last a medium close-up of him looking anxiously around, with the fluorescent lights now out of focus. In an exterior shot of the car park (the camera subtly repositioned from the first Deep Throat scene), the reporter climbs the stairs to ground level. Appearing apprehensive in full shot, Woodward reaches the wet street. The music resumes, with the camera following and closing on Woodward, who breaks into a run. Abruptly, the moment's darkness is broken by a light's glare that hits his face. He whirls to see if a car is following him, his frightened response accented by a zoom at the end of the tracking shot.

And then: a shot of the empty street behind him, a medium close-up of Woodward looking, the right side of his face in darkness, and then the scene's final image, a long shot of Woodward alone at dawn, walking slowly across a large parking lot, surrounded by public buildings, with the Washington Monument in the background. The sequence has associated silence and darkness with danger. The concluding direct cut to the newsroom's bright, noisy bustle portrays the *Post*'s offices as a sanctuary.

These first two Deep Throat sequences demonstrate a film's capacity to assign meaning to potentially neutral signifiers: *ATPM* makes silence and darkness threatening, but we can easily imagine another movie doing the opposite. The third, and shortest (3′46″), of these sequences will play another instructive trick, uncoupling the prominence/significance pairing that conventional practice maintains in correlation. It begins with the previously discussed shot of Woodward running down the unidentified street. The film cuts to a close-up of the back of Woodward's head, with the surrounding area in absolute darkness. He looks off-screen right, and we get a remarkably Hopperesque image of a taxi parked at an Exxon station, presumably from his point of view. Unsettlingly, however, the shot's status immediately changes as Woodward walks into it, forcing us to redefine what we're seeing, just as another car passes behind him. A closer shot of Woodward approaching the cab is followed by a bust

shot of him looking off-screen right. The cut reveals the other car pulling up to a phone booth. The darkness and the camera's distance from it combine to obscure the features of both driver and passenger.

The movie has isolated this other car and made us notice it. Most film-making will reserve such visual (or auditory) prominence for narratively significant things, exiling the incidentals to the backgrounds and margins, where they are left to take care of themselves. The detective story's great appeal, however, derives from its insistence that *anything may be important*, a dispensation that redeems the ordinary banality of the world by summoning our attention to *everything*. Is this other car trailing Woodward? Does its presence suggest a plot against him? Who are the driver and passenger? (Note the proximity of paranoia to a detective's heightened alertness.) Here, the prominence of the other car proves misleading: it will not contribute to the story. But the movie has retuned our sensibilities, asking us not to dismiss anything too quickly. It is precisely the attitude that Watergate demanded of Woodward and Bernstein.

This third Deep Throat meeting offers other variations. Shot 10 of the sequence shows Woodward arriving at an unrecognisable place, an apparent construction site scarred by an ongoing excavation. But as the shot continues, with Woodward running to the rendezvous, we discover that the familiar multistorey car park

actually sits beside this construction project, a new camera angle
revealing it in the foreground. The moment provides an important
cinematic lesson, especially regarding *ATPM*: any frame, *like any
source*, may withhold more than it shows – something always lies off
screen. Having seen the car park's exterior twice before, we thought
we completely knew the neighbourhood. We were wrong.

The next shot shows Woodward in the car park, emerging
from the darkness and again startled from behind by Deep Throat's
voice, 'Over here.' After Woodward enters from the left darkness
and walks away from the camera back into darkness, the film cuts
to a shot of Deep Throat, with only a small part of his face visible.
The following 1'54" of the fourteen back-and-forth shots stick to the

refrain established in the first two sequences, but the two men have reversed positions: Woodward is now on the right, Deep Throat on the left, all but a small part of the right side of his face in complete darkness.

As in the second sequence, the dialogue's crucial lines are edited to coincide with the speaker's image: Woodward's with, 'Look, I'm tired of your chicken-shit games. I don't want hints. I need to know what you know'; Deep Throat's with, 'It was a Haldeman operation,' and 'Your lives are in danger.' The episode ends with Woodward entering Bernstein's apartment. 'I like going from light to dark, dark to light,' Willis acknowledged (Mikulec). Had he been in charge of *ATPM*'s soundtrack, he would have said the same thing about going from silence to noise.

Pakula made clear that he had consciously planned the film's third important dialectic:

My idea was to start the picture with no camera movement – just people sitting at telephones doing their work. Then the camera starts to move as the people become more manic, the action becomes more intense. Finally, at the end I did the longest move of the picture, a race by Redford and Hoffman the complete length of the newsroom. In a picture with so many words there is a tendency to over-use the camera. I tried not to. (Mikulec)

In Noël Burch's terms, this strategy 'consists of emphasizing one of the two poles of [an opposition] by using it rarely' (Burch 1981: 56). The cut that ends a long take, for example, will gain in importance from having been withheld; the camera movement that interrupts a long succession of static shots will inevitably seem to convey something urgent. Pakula's assistant Jon Boorstin (2016) counts 'only four tracking shots in the newsroom, all at critical moments in the story':

- Woodward and Bernstein's first exchange (when Woodward questions Bernstein about rewriting his copy)

- Bradlee's emergence from his office and his walk across the newsroom to Bernstein's desk, where he cuts their story ('You haven't got it')
- Bernstein dragging Sally Aiken to Woodward's desk to reveal that Ken Clawson had written the Canuck letter
- Woodward and Bernstein rushing through the newsroom to catch Bradlee in the elevator

While not occurring in the newsroom, the dramatic tracking shot-cum-zoom that ends Woodward's second Deep Throat interview has a similar effect, especially after the sequence's previous twenty-seven fixed-position shot/reverse shots covering their conversation. In fact, even the newsroom scenes contain other camera movements, including the first one, of Simons hurrying to Rosenfeld's office. We should also include the scenes when Woodward leaves his desk to ask Rosenfeld, 'Who's Charles Colson?', and when the two reporters walk to Bradlee's office. The famous overhead shot in the Library of Congress involves multiple camera movements, linked by two dissolves, pulling upwards a hundred feet until the reporters appear lost in the enormous space. These scenes are memorable precisely because Pakula has not been prodigal with his camera movements: he has made them count.

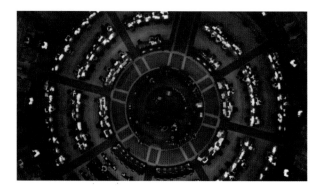

## Pairs III

The most important of the film's paired oppositions juxtaposes Woodward and Bernstein's accelerating accounts of the Watergate scandal with the other media's near-complete neglect. Warning that *The Post* may have dangerously committed itself to a dead-end, Foreign Editor Scott (John McMartin) reminds Bradlee that 'almost no other papers are reprinting our stuff', and, indeed, *ATPM* shows only *The New York Times* also regularly pursuing the story. Leonard Downie, Jr, then the *Post*'s Deputy Metro Editor, recalls the mood:

> It is hard to describe how isolated those of us working on Watergate often felt at the time. We were a relatively small number of young Metro reporters and editors without experience in federal investigations, national politics, or the workings of the White House. Our work was still being questioned by others in our own newsroom and largely ignored by much of the rest of the media. (Downie 2020: 85)

The *Post*'s publisher, Katharine Graham, had similar anxieties: 'I sometimes privately thought, if this is such a hell of a story, then where is everybody else' (Downie 2020: 85)?

In the movie, however, this contrast appears more often less as one between *The Post* and other newspapers than as one between *The Post* and television. As the reporters work at their desks, editorial office monitors display the obvious news of the day and the Nixon Administration's version of it: McGovern's announcement of Eagleton's withdrawal from his vice-presidential candidacy; Ford's declaration of Nixon's renomination; the explicit denials and sophistic equivocations of Kleindienst, Agnew, Ziegler and MacGregor; Nixon's second-term swearing-in. In fact, television began catching up to Woodward and Bernstein only when CBS's Walter Cronkite, over four months after the break-in, devoted exactly half of two consecutive show's total forty-four minutes to the story. *ATPM* acknowledges this late arrival on the scene. Manically telling Woodward about his interview with the Bookkeeper, Bernstein says,

Boy, that woman was paranoid. At one point, I suddenly wondered how high up this thing goes, and her paranoia finally got to me. I thought that what we had was so hot that at any moment, CBS or NBC were gonna come in through the windows and take the story away.

'She's afraid of John Mitchell,' Woodward replies, 'and you're afraid of Walter Cronkite.'

While the Foreign Editor's scepticism makes explicit the *Post*'s own internal debate about their story's legitimacy, Pakula was not content to leave matters there. *ATPM*'s power depends on making the viewer *feel* this conflict as the atmosphere in which Woodward and Bernstein worked. Thus, as Felipe González Silva (2021) notes, Pakula 'assembles the film as a dispute between forces competing for control of the audio-visual space', creating a world 'where different sound and image sources fight for attention'. This contrast sometimes appears in the deep-focus photography cinematographer Gordon Willis used for the newsroom sequences, where the evenly lit, bright space afforded possibilities for playing off background reporters pursuing their own stories against the foreground of Woodward and Bernstein's Watergate work. Even more effective, however, are scenes involving a split diopter.

A film, as Godard reminds us, is composed of sounds and images, but they present the film-maker with different possibilities. While almost every movie soundscape results from the careful mixing of multiple tracks, a director can typically show only one image at a time. Attaching a split diopter (a half-convex glass) to a camera's lens makes one side of the lens near-sighted and the other far-sighted. Instead of an image with a continuous depth of field, the split diopter produces one divided between shallow and deep focus, juxtaposed in the same frame – in effect, two images at once. With the split diopter, a film-maker can combine two or more stories on the soundtrack with two on the image track. We can see this effect in one of *ATPM*'s most important scenes, the six-minute take of Woodward's phone conversations with Kenneth Dahlberg (CREEP's Midwest Finance Chairman) and Clark MacGregor (Nixon's Campaign Chairman).

The shot begins (47:56) with Woodward at his desk in the right foreground, while to the left of a white column that divides the image in half, reporters gather around a television broadcasting McGovern's announcement that he has asked his vice-presidential candidate, Missouri senator Thomas Eagleton, to withdraw from the race. The shot's right half is in shallow focus, with the woman at the desk immediately behind Woodward already blurry. The image's left side, however, sharply renders the reporters in the background. From the shot's beginning, the camera is moving, almost imperceptibly, closer to Woodward.

The image's two halves, each with its own sounds, compete for our interest. McGovern's voice is loud and clear: 'The public debate about Senator Eagleton's past medical history [previous hospitalisations for depression] continue to divert attention from the great national issues that need to be discussed.' Pakula has manipulated the sound to stage the contrast: we can readily hear the television in the deep background, but not a reporter speaking to the woman seated immediately behind Woodward. As Woodward reaches Dahlberg, we hear McGovern announcing that he has asked for Eagleton's withdrawal, and reporters around the television signal others to join them, gathering a group of fifteen, which includes the Foreign Editor, Kay Eddy and Sally Aiken. The neglected Watergate story, represented by the Dahlberg conversation, now begins to

drown out the television, and (at 49:15) the group around the
monitor breaks up as Woodward's questioning sharpens: 'How
do you think your check got into the bank account of a Watergate
burglar?' At 49:44, Dahlberg hangs up.

At 50:04, as Woodward calls MacGregor, the increasingly
tighter shot of Woodward leaves only one or two people in the left
background. The image has become a close-up of Woodward, and
as MacGregor warns him (51:08), 'if you print that [the fact that
MacGregor knows how Dahlberg's cheque got into a burglar's
account], our relationship will be terminated', the shot shows
*only* Woodward. After gradually receding, the image's left side
has disappeared. At 51:16, the out-of-focus woman behind him

signals to Woodward that Dahlberg has called back. (Note Pakula's willingness to be inconsistent: he allows this woman to be heard, but when he needed to stage the contrast between the Eagleton story and Watergate, he muted the reporter occupying the same place.) Dahlberg inadvertently drops a bombshell: he gave the cheque to Maurice Stans, Nixon's Finance Committee Chairman. At 53:30, Woodward begins typing; at 53:33, Bernstein calls.

Having won what González Silva (2021) calls 'the battle for prominence', Woodward and the Watergate story surrender it in the next shot. The redistribution of significance resumes with a television broadcasting information about Eagleton, accompanying a *Post* front page, whose large headline reads:

'Eagleton Bows Out of '72 Race; McGovern Weighs Replacement'

A hand turns the paper over to reveal the Woodward–Bernstein story's much smaller notice:

'Bug Suspect Got Campaign Funds'

Pakula returns to the split diopter in a later scene, where it again enables him to dramatise the contrast between the official news and Watergate. Rosenfeld tells Woodward and Bernstein that Stans has managed to postpone the release of the GAO's report, expected to reveal the Nixon campaign's misuse of funds. 'The grand jury indictment will stop at the five burglars, Hunt and Liddy,' he concludes. 'And that's the end of your story.' The movie cuts to a long shot of the newsroom, with a television monitor in the left mid-foreground and Woodward at his typewriter in the deep far-right. Gerald Ford is announcing the convention's vote to renominate Nixon, the television audio as loud as Woodward's typewriter, even when Pakula cuts to a medium close-up first of the reporter, and then to the article he's writing about the GAO.

At 1:12:40, the split diopter shot begins, with the TV now much larger in the foreground, and the conventioneers' chant ('Four More Years! Four More Years!') overwhelming the typewriter's sound. (Despite the apparently continuous audio, when the television image changes to show Nixon at 1:13:12, a barely detectable jump cut on Woodward indicates a splice.) The official story seems to have won out. But the sequence ends by reasserting Watergate's priority: a close-up of the teletype machine entering Woodward's story ironically comments on Nixon's remarks, heard simultaneously on the soundtrack:

Wonderful young faces I see out there. Your enthusiasm, your idealism, your hard work. This is your first vote, and years from now, I just hope you can all look back and say it was one of your best votes.

*ATPM*'s final scene again deploys the split diopter to present, for the last time, the contest between the two stories. Having been chastised by Bradlee for their mistakes, Woodward and Bernstein appear alone in the newsroom's background, at work on their typewriters. The film dissolves to a shot of the same workspace, now fully occupied, with a monitor in the foreground showing Nixon's swearing-in. Woodward and Bernstein ignore it, and the camera closes in, with the television now in the left foreground and the reporters in the rear to the right. We can now detect the split diopter effect as the reporters behind the monitor fall out of focus. Even when the camera moves still closer, eventually cutting to a medium shot of the reporters at their desks, the inauguration sounds dominate, threatening to drown out the persistent typewriters. Only when the film concludes, with images of teletypes reporting Nixon's resignation and the perpetrators' sentencing, do Woodward and Bernstein triumph. The two stories, so long on parallel tracks, have finally converged. The reporters' story has become the permanent one.

# Chronology of Events Portrayed in
## All the President's Men

**1 June 1972**
· Nixon returns from Moscow, addresses Joint Session of Congress.

**17 June 1972**
· 2.30 am: Five men arrested in Watergate burglary of Democratic National Headquarters. *Washington Post* reporter Al Lewis phones in the details.
· 9.00 am: Woodward woken by *Post* editor, told to go to that afternoon's arraignment of the burglars.
· 6.30 pm: at *Post* deadline for Sunday edition, eight reporters file story on break-in under byline of *Post*'s Al Lewis.

**18 June 1972**
· Watergate burglary story on Sunday *Post* front page.
· Bernstein rewrites Woodward's story on the suspects, improving it.
· Associated Press story that James McCord, one of the burglars, had been Security Coordinator for CREEP.
· After midnight, Woodward gets call from *Post* night police reporter telling him that two of the burglars' address books contain the name of Howard Hunt and 'W. House' or 'W.H'.

**19 June 1972**
· Deep Throat confirms Hunt's involvement in break-in.

· At 3.00 pm, Woodward calls White House and asks for Hunt, who is linked to Charles Colson (Special Counsel to the President).
· Woodward reaches Hunt at Mullen public relations firm.
· Woodward calls Ken Clawson, White House Director of Communications, who, without being asked, denies White House participation in burglary.
· Woodward learns from Robert Bennett, president of Mullen, that Hunt had worked for the CIA.
· First *Post* story with Woodward–Bernstein joint byline.

**20 June 1972**
· Woodward's story linking Hunt to Colson and the White House appears in *The Post*. White House Press Secretary denies any Administration involvement.

**22 June 1972**
· Nixon issues first public denial of any White House involvement.

**1 July 1972**
· Former Attorney General John Mitchell resigns as manager of Nixon re-election campaign.

Sometime in this period:
· Bernstein telephones young woman who had once worked for a Colson

assistant, learns that Hunt was investigating Ted Kennedy.
· Bernstein calls White House Librarian, who denies knowing Hunt.
· Woodward and Bernstein go to Library of Congress.
· Bradlee edits story on Hunt: 'You haven't got it.'

### 7 July 1972
· Hunt surrenders to police; *Post* runs story on Hunt investigating Kennedy at Chappaquiddick.
· Story stalls: Bradlee on vacation until mid-August.

### 22 July 1972
· Woodward goes on vacation.
· *Newsday* reports that former White House aide Gordon Liddy has been fired by Mitchell for refusing to answer FBI questions about burglary.

### 25 July 1972
· *New York Times* front-page story describing fifteen phone calls from one of the burglars to CREEP.
· In call to phone company contact, Bernstein learns that the burglar's phone records have been subpoenaed by Miami State's Attorney and his chief investigator, Martin Dardis.

### 31 July 1972
· Bernstein goes to Miami, learns of a $25,000 cashiers cheque payable to Kenneth Dahlberg.
· McGovern announces Eagleton's withdrawal from race.
· Woodward phones Dahlberg at night; Dahlberg reports giving cheque to either Hugh Sloan (CREEP Treasurer) or Maurice Stans

(Secretary of Commerce and CREEP Finance Chairman).
· Woodward telephones CREEP Chairman Clark MacGregor, who denies any knowledge.

### 1 August 1972
· Woodward's story on Dahlberg appears in *Post* byline shared by Bernstein.
· Woodward calls Dahlberg again.
· Woodward calls General Accounting Office, which announces CREEP audit.
· Sloan refuses to talk to a *Post* reporter.

Sometime in next few days:
· GAO reports hundreds of thousands of unaccounted dollars in CREEP slush fund.
· Bernstein learns that Liddy will take the blame for burglary.

### 16 August 1972
· MacGregor shifts blame to Liddy, warns Woodward, 'If you print that [that MacGregor knew about the events], our relationship will be terminated.'

### Mid-August
· *Post* researcher obtains list of CREEP employees; Woodward and Bernstein begin house-to-house visits in attempt to interview those listed. First person Bernstein visits is a terrified woman ('I know you're only trying to do your job, but you don't realize the pressure we're under').

### 21 August 1972
· Republican Convention begins.

**22 August 1972**
- GAO reports audit's release delayed by Stans.
- Nixon renominated.

**26 August 1972**
- GAO audit released, announcing possible violation of campaign financing laws.

**29 August 1972**
- Nixon announces possible 'technical violations' of campaign financing laws, attributable to both parties.
- *Post* article reporting that Hunt, Liddy, Sans, Sloan and Mitchell under investigation.

**14 September 1972**
- Bernstein interviews CREEP Bookkeeper (Judy Hoback Miller) and Hugh Sloan.

**15 September 1972**
- Hunt, Liddy and the five Watergate burglars indicted.
- Justice Department announces end of investigation.

**16 September 1972**
- On the telephone, Deep Throat tells Woodward that the story he is writing, which links Watergate burglary to CREEP officials, is 'too soft' and should mention other covert actions. Bernstein writes a story linking burglary to John Mitchell.

**17 September 1972**
- Woodward and Bernstein go together to the Bookkeeper's house.
- Back at *The Post*, Woodward telephones Deep Throat, who seems frightened. He warns Woodward of the situation's growing danger, saying he would no longer speak about it on the phone.

**18 September 1972**
- Bernstein makes first visit to Hugh Sloan, at his house in McLean, VA. He reveals John Mitchell's complicity and his own trouble finding a new job ('I've been in the papers too much').

**28 September 1972**
- Woodward and Bernstein both visit Sloan, who provides more information about CREEP's slush fund and Mitchell.
- Bernstein telephones a source who confirms the reporters' prospective story.
- At 11.30 pm, Bernstein telephones Mitchell, who denies story, warning that 'Katie Graham's [*Post* publisher] gonna get her tit caught in a wringer.'
- Reached at home, Bradlee authorises Bernstein to print the story.
- Bernstein gets tip linking covert activities to Donald Segretti.

**5 October 1972**
- *Post* freelancer Robert Meyers visits Segretti in Marina del Ray, CA; he refuses to talk, but Bernstein has uncovered information about him, especially his connection to Nixon aide Dwight Chapin.

**9 October 1972**
- Woodward meets Deep Throat in Rosslyn, VA, multistorey car park. He confirms involvement of Mitchell, Ehrlichman and the White House.

- Bernstein learns from Marilyn Berger (Sally Aiken in the film) that Ken Clawson wrote the Canuck letter, ending Muskie's candidacy. Bradlee and other *Post* editors believe her story, despite Clawson's denial.

## 10 October 1972

- *Post* front-page story, 'FBI Finds Nixon Aides Sabotaged Democrats'. Story mentions Segretti's involvement.
- *Post* front-page story on Clawson as the author of the Canuck letter, accompanied by Administration's denial.

## 15 and 16 October 1972

- *Post* stories link Segretti to Chapin and Herbert Kalmbach, Nixon's personal lawyer.

## 16 October 1972

- Nixon Press Secretary, Ron Ziegler, describes *Post* stories as 'based on hearsay, innuendo, guilt by association'. Bradlee stands by *Post* stories.

## 19 October 1972

- Woodward and Bernstein front-page story describing 'massive campaign of political spying and sabotage', directed by the White House and CREEP.

## 20 October 1972

- Woodward meets Deep Throat again in the car park. He refuses to discuss Haldeman.
- Bernstein's FBI source tells him, 'You guys are causing big trouble. Our reports are showing up in the paper almost verbatim. ... Except for Mitchell. We didn't have that.'

## 23 October 1972

- Woodward and Bernstein visit Sloan, who approves their writing about Haldeman's involvement: 'I have no problems if you write a story like that.'
- Asked to get another confirmation, Bernstein talks to a source who seems to confirm Sloan's account.

## 25 October 1972

- *Post* story links Haldeman to CREEP secret fund.
- Press Secretary Ziegler denies Sloan implicated Haldeman in grand jury testimony. He had not been asked.
- On television, Sloan's lawyer says that Sloan had not named Haldeman to the grand jury. He does not say that Sloan had not been asked about Haldeman. Bradlee described the resulting criticism of *The Post* as 'my lowest moment in Watergate'.

## 26 October 1972

- For the last time until late January 1973, Woodward meets in the car park with Deep Throat, who scolds him, 'Haldeman slipped away from you. ... this whole business is a Haldeman operation. ... You've got people feeling sorry for Haldeman. I didn't think that was possible.'
- Woodward writes story quoting Deep Throat anonymously.
- CREEP Chairman MacGregor acknowledges existence of fund, but denies its secrecy.

## 11 November 1972

- Bernstein flies to California to meet with Segretti, who admits being hired by Chapin, but he refuses to go on the record.

## Subsequent events

**8 January 1973**
· Hunt pleads guilty to burglary and bugging.

**20 January 1973**
· Nixon inaugurated for second term.

**31 January 1973**
· Liddy and McCord convicted.

**7 February 1973**
· Senate Watergate Committee established.

**23 March 1973**
· Judge John J. Sirica publishes a letter from imprisoned McCord reporting Administration pressure to plead guilty and say nothing.

**30 April 1973**
· Haldeman and Ehrlichman resign.
· Nixon fires John Dean and Attorney General Kleindienst.

**1 May 1973**
· Press Secretary Ziegler apologises to *The Post* and to Woodward and Bernstein.

**16 May 1973**
· On the eve of the Senate Watergate Committee's first session, Deep Throat warns Woodward that 'Everyone's life is in danger.'

**17 May 1973**
· Watergate Committee begins hearings, which run until August.

**22 June 1973**
· Mark Felt (Deep Throat) retires from the FBI.
· Woodward and Bernstein on leave writing *All the President's Men*.

**10 October 1973**
· Vice President Agnew resigns. Nixon appoints Gerald Ford to the office.

**12 October 1973**
· Federal Appeals Court orders release of White House tapes.

**20 October 1973**
· Saturday Night Massacre: Secretary of State Elliot Richardson refuses to fire Special Prosecutor Archibald Cox, as does his deputy William Rucklehaus. Both resign. Nixon's Solicitor General Bork fires Cox.

**1 March 1974**
· Haldeman, Ehrlichman and Mitchell indicted. Nixon named as co-conspirator.

**15 June 1974**
· *All the President's Men* published.

**24 June 1974**
· US Supreme Court orders release of White House tapes, which contain conclusive evidence of Nixon's complicity.

**8 August 1974**
· President Nixon resigns.

# Credits

**All the President's Men**
USA
1976

**Production Companies**
Warner Bros. presents
A Wildwood Enterprises
production
A Robert Redford–Alan J.
Pakula film
**Directed by**
Alan J. Pakula
**Produced by**
Walter Coblenz
**Screenplay by**
William Goldman
based on the book by
Carl Bernstein and Bob
Woodward
**Music by**
David Shire
**Production Designer**
George Jenkins
**Film Editor**
Robert L. Wolfe, A.C.E.
**Director of Photography**
Gordon Willis, A.S.C.
**Associate Producers**
Michael Britton
Jon Boorstin
**Casting**
Alan Shayne
**Casting Consultant**
Isabel Halliburton
**Executive Production
Manager**
E. Darrell Hallenbeck
**First Assistant Directors**
Bill Green
Art Levinson
**Script Supervisor**

Karen Hale Wookey
(as Karen Wookey)
**Set Decoration by**
George Gaines
**Second Assistant
Directors**
Charles Ziarko
Kim Kurumada
**Camera Operator**
Ralph Gerling
**First Assistant
Cameraman**
Ray De La Motte
(as Ray de la Motte)
**Second Assistant
Cameramen**
Ron Vargas
Peter Salim
**Supervising Sound
Editor**
Milton C. Burrow
**Music Editor**
Nicholas C. Washington
**Assistant Editors**
Carroll Timothy O'Meara
(as Tim O'Meara)
Steve Potter
**Title Design**
Dan Perri
**Key Grip**
Bob Rose
**Best Boy**
Carl R. Gibson, Jr
(as Carl Gibson, Jr)
**Crab Dolly Grip**
Frank Lambers
**Assistant Art Director**
Robert I. Jillson
(as Bob Jillson)
**Draftsman**
George Szeptycki

(as J. George Szeptycki)
**Lead Man**
Mike Higelmire
**Construction
Coordinator**
Robert Krume
**Construction Foreman**
Roger Irvin
**Special Effects**
Henry Millar
**Key Make-up Artist**
Gary Liddiard
**Make-up Artists**
Fern Buchner
Don L. Cash
(as Don Cash)
**Hairdressers**
Romaine Greene
Lynda Gurasich
**Research**
Steve Bussard
de Forest Research Inc.
**Gaffer**
George Holmes
**Best Boy Electric**
Larry D. Howard
(as Larry Howard)
**Auditor**
Ken Ryan
**Production Sound
Mixers**
James E. Webb
(as Jim Webb)
Les Fresholtz
**Boom Men**
Chris McLaughlin
Clint Althouse
**Rerecording Mixers**
Arthur Piantadosi
(as Art Piantadosi)
Les Fresholtz

Dick Alexander
**Property Masters**
Alan Levine
(as Allan Levine)
Bill MacSems
(as Bill Mac Sems)
**Assistant Property Masters**
Matty Azzarone
Guy Bushman
**Costume Supervisor**
Bernie Pollack
**Assistant Costumers**
Jules Melillo
G. Perez
**Transportation Coordinator**
Craig Pinkard
**Transportation Captain**
Edward Baken
(as Eddie Baken)
**Production Coordinators**
Rebecca Britton
Erika Koppitz
Ronnie Kramer
**Production Assistant**
Buck Holland
**Production Staff**
Eve Christopher
Phil Geyelin
Jill Gifford
Marge Leonard
John Bard Manulis
(as John Manulis)
Stuart Neumann
(as Stuart Newman)
Tammy Pittman
Liz Shea
Shirley Street
**Location Manager**

Steve Vetter
**Still Men**
Howard L. Bingham
(as Howard Bingham)
Louis Goldman
**Production Publicist**
Jack Hirshberg
**Unit Publicist**
Joanna Ney
**Publicity Consultant**
Lois Smith

**CAST (Main)**
**Dustin Hoffman**
Carl Bernstein
**Robert Redford**
Bob Woodward
**Jack Warden**
Harry Rosenfeld
**Martin Balsam**
Howard Simons
**Hal Holbrook**
Deep Throat
**Jason Robards**
Ben Bradlee
**Jane Alexander**
Bookkeeper
**Meredith Baxter**
Debbie Sloan
**Ned Beatty**
Dardis
**Stephen Collins**
Hugh Sloan
**Penny Fuller**
Sally Aiken
**John McMartin**
Foreign Editor
**Robert Walden**
Donald Segretti
**Frank Wills**
Frank Wills

**Lindsay Ann Crouse**
**(as Lindsay Crouse)**
Kay Eddy
**Valerie Curtin**
Betty Milland
**Nicolas Coster**
**(as Nicholas Coster)**
Markham
**Polly Holliday**
Dardis's secretary
**David Arkin**
Eugene Bachinski
**Jess Osuna**
Joe, FBI agent
**Penny Peyser**
Sharon Lyons
**Paul Lambert**
National Editor
**Allyn Ann McLerie**
Carolyn Abbott
**James Murtaugh**
Congress Library Clerk
**Jaye Stewart**
male librarian

**Production Details**
Colour (Technicolor)
35mm
1.85:1
Running time:
138 minutes

**Release Details**
US theatrical release on
9 April 1976 by Warner
Bros.
UK theatrical release
on 29 April 1976 by
Columbia-Warner
Distributors

# Bibliography

*All the President's Men*. Dir. Alan J. Pakula, Warner Home Video, 2011.

Barthes, Roland (1974). *S/Z*, trans. Richard Miller. New York: Hill & Wang.

Bernstein, Carl and Bob Woodward (1974). *All the President's Men*. New York: Simon & Schuster.

Bernstein, Carl and Bob Woodward (1975). Written notes and typed memo to Robert Redford. Cinephilia and Filmmaking. Available at: <https://cinephiliabeyond.tumblr.com/post/67516174949/written-notes-and-typed-memo-to-robert-redford> (accessed 6 August 2021).

Bonitzer, Pascal (1981). 'Partial Vision: Film and the Labyrinth'. *Wide Angle* 4 no. 4: 56–63.

Boorstin, Jon (1995). *Making Movies Work: Thinking Like a Filmmaker*. Los Angeles: Silman-James Press.

Boorstin, Jon (2016). 'On Its 40th Anniversary: Notes on the Making of *All the President's Men*'. *Los Angeles Review of Books*. Available at: <https://lareviewofbooks.org/article/on-its-40th-anniversary-notes-on-the-making-of-all-the-presidents-men/> (accessed 24 July 2021).

Bordwell, David (1985). *Narration in the Fiction Film*. Madison: University of Wisconsin Press.

Brooks, Van Wyck (1966). *Writers at Work: The Paris Review Interviews, Second Series*. New York: The Viking Press.

Brown, Jared (2005). *Alan J. Pakula: His Films and His Life*. New York: Back Stage Books.

Burch, Noël (1979). *To the Distant Observer: Form and Meaning in the Japanese Cinema*. Berkeley: University of California Press.

Burch, Noël (1980). 'Carl Theodor Dreyer: The Major Phase'. In Richard Roud, *Cinema: A Critical Dictionary*. New York: The Viking Press.

Burch, Noël (1981). *Theory of Film Practice*, trans. Helen R. Lane. Princeton, NJ: Princeton University Press.

Burrow, Colin (2021). 'Ti tum ti tum ti tum'. *London Review of Books* 43 no. 19 (7 October).

Cavell, Stanley (1979). *The World Viewed*. Cambridge, MA: Harvard University Press.

Cieslikowski, Craig (2021). 'You're Missing the Overall'. Unpublished paper.

Downie, Jr, Leonard (2020). *All About the Story: News, Power, Politics, and the Washington Post*. New York: PublicAffairs.

Forster, E. M. (1985). *Aspects of the Novel*. New York: Harvest.

Gaynor, Michael J. (2016). 'All the President's Men: An Oral History, Washingtonian (3 April). Available at: <https://www.washingtonian.com/216.04/03/all-the-presidents-men-movie-oral-history/> (accessed 28 November 2021).

Glock, Hans-Johan (2004). 'Was Wittgenstein an Analytic Philosopher?' *Metaphilosophy* 35 no. 4: 419–44.

Goldman, William (1997). *Five Screenplays*. New York: Applause Books.

González Silva, Felipe (2021). 'Audio-Visual Découpage in *All the President's Men*'. Unpublished paper.

Hirshberg, Jack (1976). *A Portrait of All the President's Men*. New York: Warner Books.

Holmes, Nathan. 'Deep Backgrounds: Landscapes of Labor in *All the President's Men*'. *Imaginations* 9 no. 1 (2018): 87–107.

Knudsen, Matt (2021). '*All the President's Men*: Lighting in the Three Deep Throat Scenes'. Unpublished paper.

Kraft, Elizabeth (2008). '*All the President's Men* as a Woman's Film'. *Journal of Popular Film and Television* 36 no. 1: 30–7.

Marx, Samuel (1975). *Mayer and Thalberg: The Make-Believe Saints*. Hollywood: Samuel French.

Mendieta, Eduardo, ed. (2005). *Take Care of Freedom and Truth Will Take Care of Itself: Interviews with Richard Rorty*. Palo Alto, CA: Stanford University Press.

Mikulec, Sven (n.d). '*All the President's Men*: Following the Money to Become One of the Most Remarkable American Films to Date'. *Cinephilia & Beyond*. Available at: <https://cinephiliabeyond.org/presidents-men-following-money-become-one-remarkable-american-films-date/> (accessed 14 November 2021).

Naremore, James (1988). *Acting in the Cinema*. Berkeley: University of California Press.

Orlando, Jordan (2018). 'William Goldman Turned Reporters into Heroes in *All the President's Men*. *The New Yorker* (21 November).

Perkins, V. F. (1993). *Film as Film*. New York: Da Capo Press.

Pye, Douglas (2000). 'Movies and Point of View'. *Movie* 36 (Winter): 2–34.

Vaughan, Dai (1999). *For Documentary*. Berkeley: University of California Press.

Willis, Gordon (1976). 'Some Unseen Cinematographic Techniques Applied to the Filming of a Best-Selling Book about a Crucial Moment in Recent American History'. *American Cinematographer* (May). Available at: <https://ascmag.com/articles/flashback-all-the-presidents-men> (accessed 7 July 2021).

Wilson, George (1986). *Narration in Light: Studies in Cinematic Point of View*. Baltimore, MD: Johns Hopkins University Press.

Wittgenstein, Ludwig (1958). *Philosophical Investigations*, trans. G. E. M. Anscombe. New York: Macmillan.

Wood, James (2019). *How Fiction Works*. New York: Vintage.

Woodward, Bob (2005). *The Secret Man: The Story of Watergate's Deep Throat*. New York: Simon & Schuster.